Thoreau's
MAINE WOODS
Yesterday and Today

THOREAU'S
MAINE WOODS

Yesterday and Today

By Cheryl Seal

Photographs by Robert F. Bukaty

YANKEE BOOKS

Emmaus, Pennsylvania

Printed in the United States of America on acid-free ∞ paper
Editor: Nan K. Smith
Book and Cover Designer: Jerry O'Brien

The authors would like to thank G. Michael de Lesseps and Dick Durrance for their assistance with photo editing.

Library of Congress Cataloging-in-Publication Data

Seal, Cheryl, 1951–
    Thoreau's Maine woods: yesterday and today / by Cheryl Seal : photographs by Robert F. Bukaty.
        p.   cm.
    Includes excerpts from the journals of Thoreau.
    ISBN 0-89909-314-0 hardcover
    1. Piscataquis County (Me.)—Description and travel. 2. Maine—Description and travel. 3. Thoreau, Henry David, 1817–1862—Journeys—Maine. 4. Thoreau, Henry David, 1817–1862—Quotations. 5. Authors, American—19th century—Journeys—Maine. 6. Authors, American—19th century—Quotations.   I. Bukaty, Robert F., 1961–. II. Thoreau, Henry David, 1817–1862. Journal. Selections. 1992. III. Title.
    F27.P5T43 1992
    917.4104'3—dc20   90-47021
                                                                CIP

Distributed in the book trade by St. Martin's Press

2 4 6 8 10 9 7 5 3 1   hardcover

CONTENTS

INTRODUCTION

The Maine Woods.

The phrase evokes an image of unbroken forest, isolated waterways, and solitude. But in reality, it is getting harder each year to find any true wilderness in Maine—or anywhere else. Since 1970, paper companies and other landowners have sliced nearly twenty thousand miles of roads through the Maine Woods, rendering nearly every niche of forest land accessible to the automobile or truck. The Allagash River, once synonymous with wilderness, is now rafted by nearly twenty thousand tourists annually, while hundreds of people each day of the summer climb Mount Katahdin. The shores of the remote St. John River are now dotted by commercial campsites, and Mount Kineo, an ancient wilderness landmark, has been subdivided for development. No place in the Maine Woods is more than two miles from a road (as one paper company spokesperson has asserted); no location is beyond the sound of chain saws. Yet against all odds, a forest, however besieged by "progress," still exists in this corner of the world. Within it still are all the threads of life that form the fabric of any forest on earth.

As we stand on the edge of the twenty-first century, facing environmental crises that threaten the survival of life on earth, we can no longer afford to think only in terms of superficially imposed political boundaries. We must realize that the world is a single ecosystem, a global environment, and that we must be its stewards. The Maine Woods is part of the global forest and reflects the problems of forests—and the natural environment—everywhere. Therefore, it is to the forest that this book is dedicated.

The quotes in the text are taken from Thoreau's journals, written from 1837 to 1862.

PART ONE

Thoreau's Forest

THE FOREST ENVIRONMENT

Who shall describe the inexpressible tenderness and immortal life of the grim forest, where Nature, though it be in mid-winter, is ever in her spring, where the moss-grown and decaying trees are not old, but seem to enjoy a perpetual youth . . . ?

The earth's forests are living vessels of the stuff of life: sunlight, earth, and water. Each acre of forest can collect at least twice as much moisture from the earth and sky as one acre of grassland. The dense green canopy filters the fall of rain to a mist that settles gently on the earth and slowly percolates down through the soil. The excess water works its way to the rocky layers below, and eventually, thoroughly purified, finds its way into streams, lakes, and rivers. The rest of the moisture is collected by the canopy and "breathed" back into the atmosphere or conducted deep into the ground by trunks and roots.

High above the forest floor, the chlorophyll-rich crowns of the trees ripple in the wind. Each needle, each leaf, hungrily soaks up the sun's light, trapping its energy. As much as thirty percent of all light striking the earth in regions that support plant life is absorbed at least temporarily by plants. Without this primary resource of energy, few other forms of life on the planet would be possible. And there is no more efficient solar panel than the thick, living, green roof of a forest.

Far below, the roots of the forest probe beneath the topsoil, tapping the minerals and water locked there and drawing them into the body of the trees, from which they will eventually be released again.

The forest is also a natural air filter. Dust and other impurities are trapped in the needles and leaves of trees. The air is kept well humidified by the water vapor released into the atmosphere from the forest canopy. A single tree releases abundant oxygen—enough to keep a family of four alive for a year. In fact, all the oxygen now present in the atmosphere has been released by plants.

The forest is, perhaps above all, a source of life renewed through death. The trees are living silos of nutrients and energy ultimately released through decay. As a tree begins the slow process of dying, fungi begin to grow on its bark in rosettes of yellow and orange or in thick shelves of white and gray-brown. A cubic meter of air contains millions of fungal spores ready to alight and do their vital work. Their threadlike "roots," called *hyphae,* penetrate deep into the wood, slowly digesting it, opening breaches in the tough outer wall through which the hidden army of the forest floor, the detritus eaters, can swarm. Soon, the dead tree is a crowded colony of bacteria, beetles, and worms. Dead trees also become the natural habitat for a legion of other forest animals—woodpeckers, owls, mice, snakes, weasels, and rabbits. As many as four hundred different species of vertebrate and invertebrate animals living in the eastern forest of the United States make use of dead and dying trees for shelter, food, storage, perching, and hiding.

Over time, the roots and branches of a dying tree become weaker and more brittle. Eventually the limbs snap in the wind, or the entire tree gives up its grip upon the soil and crashes to the forest floor or into the arms of its living neighbors. As decay becomes complete, the trunks, stumps, and branches become softened mounds continuous with the earth, covered by a carpet of green moss or a layer of dead leaves, their lifetime savings of energy and nutrients diffused into the rest of the forest. Each tree ultimately returns perhaps as much as twice as many nutrients to the environment as it takes in during its entire lifespan. From this generous "interest," new life can spring.

HIGHEST AND BEST USE

What a place to live, what a place to die and be buried in! There, certainly, men would live forever and laugh at death and the grave.

In the course of the last million years, four successive waves of ice have flowed and retreated over nearly half the globe. During the last wave, which ended approximately fifteen thousand years ago, all of the region now known as Maine was crushed beneath a frozen river of ice and compacted snow more than a mile thick, so dense and heavy that the earth's crust was sunken. For thousands of years, the landscape was a silent, solid ocean of white.

The ice receded slowly. In its wake, it left a scarred, boulder-strewn landscape nearly as barren as the moon. But not for long. Life, ever tenacious, began to creep back, even in the glacier's shadow. Tundra was the first to form. Lichens clung to the rocks like frost in fragile patterns of dusty gray-green, blue, and pink. Soon, a low, sheltering mat of moss and grass was woven across the empty expanse, securing the thin layer of rock-milled sand and glacial till. Nourished by the decay from this

living blanket, scrubby colonies of willow and alder began to grow in flattened thickets. Next, wind-stunted clumps of spruce appeared. Within a few hundred years of the glacier's retreat, the great northern forest had regained much of its lost territory. It stretched in a sea of deep blue-green from the shores of the Atlantic to the Yukon. The soil was still thin, a fragile crust beneath an ever-deepening cushion of needles, leaves, and other plant litter. It took—and still takes—a thousand years for a single inch of topsoil to form.

As forest life crept back into the north, nomadic bands migrated across the continent. These hunters presumably came across the land bridge that for a time joined North America to Asia across the Bering Strait. They eventually reached what is now Maine and the Maritime provinces of Canada about twelve thousand years ago. They were skilled hunters who created from stone and bones the special spear tips needed to kill their prey: caribou, giant beaver, migratory birds, fish, and perhaps muskoxen. Their descendants, who lived about five thousand years before the present, are popularly known as the Red Paint People because of the red ochre they liberally used in religious rites. They settled along the ocean shore and hunted sea mammals and swordfish. After them came other hunter-gatherers who also did some primitive farming. They eventually became the Abenaki, the "People of the Dawn." The Abenaki (or Wabanaki) comprised several Indian groups, including the tribes that still exist today in northern New England and the Maritimes: Passamaquoddy, Maliseet, Micmac, and Penobscot. The Abenaki lived most of the year along rivers in wigwams made of bark. In summer many of the tribes migrated to the coast, where the insects were less troublesome and the warm season was longer. At the time of contact with the Europeans, they were cultivating small gardens of corn, squash, beans, and melons, and they were fishing and gathering mussels, clams, and other shellfish.

The mammoths and other ice-age mammals that had lingered after the last glacier's retreat had disappeared as the climate warmed. Now the forest was full of smaller mammals, such as rabbit, fox, fisher, and squirrel, along with larger predators, such as lynx, bobcat, wolf, and mountain lion. It was also the land of abundant, magnificent hooved beasts: moose, elk, and caribou. The thousands of

glacier-dug lakes and ponds were filled with fish, as were the rivers and streams that drained them. Although the Abenaki's summer gardens and the fish and shellfish they smoked supplemented their diet, they looked for the most part to the forest for their survival. Nearly everything that was needed could be found within its green shadows. Bark from birch provided the hulls of canoes; the roots of black spruce provided strong, supple thread to stitch the canoes together. Deer and moose antler yielded needles and fishhooks. The burls found on the trunks of trees could be hollowed into bowls. Sphagnum moss made soft, absorbent diapers; berries and roots provided food and dyes; herbs provided spices and medicines. "Never had Solomon his mansion better regulated and provided with food," the Jesuit priest Pierre Biard was to exclaim in the early seventeenth century, when he lived near the Abenaki.

Trees were viewed by the Abenaki as possessing a spirit as real as that of a human. When bark was girdled from a birch for a canoe or a maple or oak felled for firewood, it was necessary to ask forgiveness of the tree's spirit and to thank it for its life-sustaining donation. Indians considered it an act of respect and appreciation to use as much of the sacrificial animal or plant as possible. Often the few remains were returned to their natural setting. The Indians viewed themselves as forest creatures, the same as the beavers that labored over their dams, the deer that foraged in the meadow, or the wolf pack that stalked its game as a close-knit family. Private ownership of land was alien. The land was there for all beasts and plants to share, although there were clearly delineated hunting and foraging territories. The lynx had a range that it defended from other large predators; the squirrel scolded any beast, large or small, that came too close to its tree; even the seagulls on their rocky islands defended a tiny patch of turf.

But such boundaries were fluid, shifting with natural conditions—even the seasons—as the needs of the community changed. The Indians believed that if one creature became too greedy, its greed would ultimately come back to haunt it and the entire community. Therefore, when Abenaki gathered roots and berries or shellfish or hunted beaver and rabbit, they made sure to leave plenty behind.

HIDEOUS BUT BOUNTIFUL WILDERNESS

For one that comes with a pencil to sketch or sing, a thousand come with an axe or rifle.

By the fifteenth century, parts of Europe had become overcrowded. Many of her great forests had been wasted, her soil worked to prostration, and many of her natural resources depleted. Ninety-five percent of the population struggled to eke out a subsistence for themselves from anemic land and to support the remaining five percent who lived in luxury. Firewood, game—even clean drinking water—were becoming scarce. In this exhausted "Old World," poverty, disease, and religious and political conflicts had become a grim but accepted way of life. As the resources dwindled, the superpowers—France, Spain, and England—vied ruthlessly for control over what was left while scrambling to find new routes to the Far East and Middle East so they might tap into fresh sources of goods and revenue. It was this quest that eventually led Christopher Columbus to stumble upon the "New World"

first seen by the Viking Leif Eriksson five hundred years before.

Dazzling reports of bounty were sent back to Europe by the North American explorers. Soon, thousands of Europeans were fired with an eagerness to make the risky three-thousand-mile leap into the unknown. But along with their new hopes and dreams, the immigrants brought with them the same approach to the land that had, over the centuries, pressed Europe to the brink of environmental bankruptcy. Conservation was unknown. Judeo-Christian doctrine commonly taught that God had given man dominion over the earth and all its resources. It was also commonly believed that wilderness was the domain of Satan, and therefore it was the duty of human beings to tame and cultivate it, thus rendering it "good." William Bradford, who arrived in the New World aboard *The Mayflower* in 1620, described the wilderness as "desolate and hideous, full of wild beasts and wild men . . . a wild and savage view." Because of the belief in the divine right of kings, European explorers had little trouble claiming vast territories of unexplored wilderness for their monarch as soon as they "discovered" it.

Captain George Weymouth sent the following report back to England after inspecting the coast of southern Maine in 1605: "In our march, we passed over very good ground, pleasant and fertile, fit for pasture, having but little wood and that oak; like stands left in the pastures of England, good and great, fit timber for any use. . . . Upon the hills grew notable high timber trees, masts for ships of four hundred tons." It was these "high timber trees"—the white pines—that made Maine so attractive. The colossal buildup of the British Navy during the sixteenth and seventeenth centuries created a greater demand for wood suitable for masts, planks, and hulls. The great oak forest that had covered England in the days of Robin Hood had been destroyed and never replanted. Softwood trees suitable for masts, such as tall, straight Scotch pines, were few and far between on the British Isles and were of inferior quality. Most shipbuilding wood had to be imported from Baltic ports a thousand miles away.

But here in the forests of the New World were the most magnificent mast pines on earth. When Weymouth gazed up at the soft blue-green spray of needles nearly two hundred feet above his helmeted head, he saw masts for men-of-war, and money. The richest stands of white pine grew conveniently along the rivers and inlets, where they could be felled easily. The pine, with its white, clear-grained wood, also made the best building lumber available anywhere. By 1650, there were dozens of sawmills in Maine (the first was built in York in 1623); the first commercial shipyard had been established (on Richmond Island in 1632); and mast landings dotted the coast.

Waste was rampant but, in the face of a seemingly endless forest, seemed insignificant. Only the trunks of most trees were taken to sawmills; the rest was burned off or left to rot. Over a hundred trees might be felled to produce two or three mast logs because the heartwood of the largest trees was often rotten. It was not until many decades later that it was discovered that the most durable wood in the forest came from the outer shell of these "rotten-hearted" trees. To soften the fall of a prime mast tree, lest its value at the English docks be reduced by damage, hundreds of smaller trees were felled just to form a "cushion." When the tall trees along the rivers' shores had been depleted and it was necessary to seek inland for the big pines, a road several yards wide and a few miles long was frequently slashed through the forest just to get at one prime tree.

Before the first permanent colony was established in New England, England had sliced up a goodly chunk of its new territory, including most of Maine, into the holdings of two business corporations known as the Plymouth and London companies. But then almost all newcomers to the New World, and to Maine, responded to its bounty with opportunism. After years of scrimping for fuel and lumber, so scarce and therefore precious in Europe, the settlers rejoiced at the sight of so many trees there for the taking. Big trees meant big houses and unlimited firewood. A big colonial home, with its inefficient fireplaces, high ceilings, and many rooms, burned thirty to forty cords of wood each year. Whole forests of hardwoods were felled and heaped in piles, then burned to make way for farms. Farmers turned their pigs and cattle loose in the forest to forage. The domestic beasts trampled the springy, mulchy soil into a muddy, compressed barnyard, stripping leaves and bark from plants, baring and gouging roots, and eating every available shoot, nut, and berry in the area. Unchecked by fences, they also trampled and devoured the small gardens of nearby Indians. In the face of such competition, game animals were driven deeper into the forest to seek new sources of food and shelter, creating yet another loss to the Indians.

Trappers saw the forest as a giant storehouse of furs, which were in high-priced demand in Europe. In just one expedition to the Maine coast in 1614, John Smith's ship pulled away with a reported eleven thousand pelts stowed in her hold. Game, in the early years of settlement, was everywhere. Travelers passing through the

woods could easily shoot a moose or caribou just to slice an evening's meal from its flank or for its hide. Partridge could be shot by the dozen along the roadside from a wagon or, later, stagecoach; squirrels, so plentiful they made the forest echo with their chatter, were used as target practice by aspiring blackpowder sharpshooters. The illusion of endless bounty was soon to be dispelled, however. By 1750, a serious firewood shortage existed in many parts of southern and coastal Maine. By as early as 1698, Massachusetts (which then included Maine) imposed a closed season on deer in an attempt to preserve the dwindling game, and "moose reeves," the forerunners of modern game wardens, were elected annually in many towns.

Maine's earliest settlement was established by George Weymouth at Popham Beach in 1608. The colony lasted only a year, but before it was disbanded Weymouth had so alienated the Indians in the region that, as one Maine historian put it, "if he had intended to render all future friendly intercourse with the Indians impossible, he could not have adopted measures better adapted to accomplish his ends." Although Weymouth's group, decimated by malnutrition and harassed by outraged natives, abandoned their settlement, others less reckless and more tenacious soon followed. By 1650, along the coast of Maine from Machias to Kittery, settlers had carved scores of homes and villages out of the forest. With ever more to come, the great change had arrived.

"*B*LOODY MAINE!"

One revelation has been made to the Indian, another to the white man. I have much to learn of the Indian, nothing of the white man.

As the lure of ready-made goods grew more seductive, the Indian turned increasingly to the white man's economic system for sustenance. He no longer hunted the beaver and the otter just to supply himself and his family with meat and warm clothing. He slaughtered them now by the thousands for the bullets, grain, and cloth of the white man.

New diseases brought by the Europeans spread through the Abenaki villages: hepatitis, smallpox—afflictions for which the Indian had no natural defenses. By 1650 in many parts of New England, including southern and coastal Maine, as much as eighty percent of the original Indian population had been wiped out by these imported diseases. It was a catastrophe proportionally more devastating than Europe's Black Death of the fourteenth century. This staggering blow to the Indian was psychological as well as physiological. Herbs and treatments, specific and suc-

cessful against long-familiar complaints, were useless against the new diseases. The people lost their faith, first in the power of their shamans and elders, then in themselves as a people. Their suffering seemed like some awful punishment. Many of the Catholic priests who lived among the Indians early on were quick to capitalize on this demoralization as a means to bring their "savage" charges to heel. White settlers often viewed the Indians' afflictions as evidence of divine intervention on their behalf. Cotton Mather was once said to have publicly thanked God for the smallpox epidemic that wiped out an entire tribe of "troublesome" Indians in the Massachusetts Bay Colony.

Throughout the seventeenth and eighteenth centuries, the French and English battled for the new continent. To the European mind, the mere use of a bountiful land was insufficient; complete possession of it was the only acceptable outcome. Nowhere was the conflict more savage than in Maine. The Abenaki were used like pawns in a deadly chess game for nearly a hundred years. Raids and massacres and counterraids and countermassacres ravaged white settlements and Indian villages alike in wave after savage wave. So vicious was this endless warring that the state's first nickname was not "The Pine Tree State" but "Bloody Maine." After the long war, the Abenaki's best lands were annexed to England without benefit of treaty or payment. When some Indians retreated to Nova Scotia, English settlers followed and soon pushed them farther on through harassment or by confiscating their property outright. There was, it seemed, nowhere for the "red man" to rest. "This land of which you wish to make yourself now absolute master," one Micmac Sagamore wrote in frustration to the English in 1749, ". . . this land belongs to me. I have come from it as certainly as the grass. . . . Show me, where I the Indian will lodge." Six years later, a forty-pound bounty was placed on the head of every adult male Indian over the age of twelve in Maine, while a twenty-pound bounty was offered for the scalp of every Indian, male or female, under the age of twelve. The red man, who at first had been willing to share the land and his knowledge freely with the outsiders from over the seas, was now hunted down.

THE TAMING OF THE WILDERNESS

*Alas for the Hunter Race! The white man has driven off
their game and substituted a cent in its place.*

By the early 1800s, the coast of Maine was settled from York to Machias and inland to Augusta. Logging operations began to push up the inland rivers to the big forest in the north. The state's waterways were the highways along which the loggers rode in search of their quarry, down which they drove it to the ever-growing number of sawmills. While the Indian had followed the waterways in a seasonal pattern that flowed with nature's cycles, the white man used the water as a means to conquer nature. Dams were built on almost every river, stream, and lake to control the flow and level of the water. Chesuncook, once a river, became a narrow lake ringed by dead trees. It was water that powered the mills that turned trees into lumber, water that carried ships laden with boards far from Maine.

Although big pine was already scarce, the settlers had quickly discovered other uses for the forest. The bark of the hemlock was a rich source of tannin used to process leather. Early on, tanning factories were built in areas where the tall, slow-growing wood was abundant. The trees were felled, then the bark from the trunks was stripped off, dried at the stump, and then hauled to the tannery on sleds in winter. The rest of the tree was left. By 1840, there were three hundred ninety-five tanneries in Maine using hemlock bark. Hemlocks do not reseed as well as other softwoods, however, and by the early part of the twentieth century, bark tannin was replaced by a chemical process. But before the tan bark era was over, an estimated nine billion board feet of hemlock had been left to rot in the forest.

In 1860 William Forster of Strong, Maine, marketed the first toothpick. Within a decade or two, whole hillsides of birches were being felled and hauled to sawmills so Americans and Europeans might better pick their teeth. Birch also was found to make good spools and dowels. By the early twentieth century, the once-common white tree that had provided the Native American with both shelter and transportation had become scarce in many areas. Yellow birch fell victim to a similar fate. When it was discovered that its outer shell made excellent veneer, the forest was soon filled with veneer loggers. Only the lower trunk of the tree was used and only the outer layer of this. Today, this gleaming, golden-skinned tree is hard to find in many areas where it was once plentiful.

The land was changing dramatically and, in some places, forever. The forest that had stood for generations of Abenaki was crashing to the ground. Without its tree cover, the climate of cleared areas in Maine grew drier and hotter. The temperature of streams denuded of the shading trees climbed as much as fifteen degrees. Many forest streams shriveled to trickles, then disappeared. Hundreds of ponds and lakes grew shallower and were choked by the algae that thrived on sun and heat. Many were turned to muddy puddles by sediment washing into them from the rapidly eroding land. As early as 1750, erosion had become a chronic problem in many settled areas. Before the coming of the white man, there were occasional forest fires, some set by the Indians to clear underbrush and drive game; but the dense green canopy, high moisture content, and wind-blocking character of the mature forest had prevented or contained the spread of most fires. The opening of the forest to farming and logging, combined with the settlers' wholesale, careless use of fire, spelled disaster for the forest. Fires swept the landscape, some of unbelievable proportions. One fire in July 1761, which started in Lebanon, New Hampshire, burned for an entire month, charring a path several miles wide all the way to the Maine coast. A year later, the same area burned again, destroying one of the largest stands of mast pines left in New England. The worst fire in Maine's history was the so-called Miramichi Fire of 1825 that started south of Mount Katahdin. Before it was over, it had burned over thirteen hundred square miles! During the eighteenth and nineteenth centuries, three-quarters of the entire state of Maine had been burned at least once.

The crops and domestic animals were draining nutrients from the cleared soil, returning little or nothing. The land, like an ill-managed bank account, dwindled steadily with too many withdrawals and too few deposits and in many regions neared bankruptcy by the second half of the 1800s.

The solution: Go west, young man . . . or woman. The newspapers became filled with ads for clippers, trains, and steamers headed west. In an 1857 issue of the *Bangor Daily Whig and Courier,* the Michigan Southern Railroad touted a record thirty-six-hour Boston to Chicago run. With unexploited acreage just for the taking in the West, Mainers could not, it seemed, get away fast enough.

PART TWO

In Search of the Maine Woods: One Man's Quest

A ROAD LESS TRAVELLED

*Now I yearn for one of those old, meandering, dry,
uninhabited roads, which lead away from towns . . .
where you may forget in what country you are travelling;
where no farmer can complain that you are treading
down his grass, no gentleman who has recently
constructed a seat in the country that you are trespassing;
. . . where the walls and fences are not cared for; where
your head is more in heaven than your feet are on earth;
. . . where you can pace when your breast is full and
cherish your moodiness . . . which the kingbird and the
swallow twitter over, and the song sparrow sings on its
rails; where the small red butterfly is at home on the
yarrow, and no boys threaten it with imprisoning hat.
There I can walk and stalk and pace and plod. . . . There
I can walk, and recover the lost child that I am without
any ringing of a bell. . . .*

When Henry David Thoreau was born, in 1817, no roads had yet been cut through the Maine Woods around Moosehead Lake, and few trees yet felled. The mighty northern forest was still a true wilderness, trod by caribou, moose, and wolves, shadowed by huge ancient trees, home to no human being—not even the Indians who passed through only in search of game.

Thoreau's native Concord was another tale. It had already passed through the "or-

deal of sheep pasturage" (as Thoreau was to later put it) and had no wildlands left—just a few hundred acres of second- and third-growth woods clumped like islands in a sea of farmland. Once the "Howling Wilderness" of *The Mayflower* veteran William Bradford, it was now a gentle, pastoral garden, lovely but tamed.

But Concord became a living classroom of natural science for Thoreau. He spent his childhood wandering through

17

her meadows, rambling in her path-threaded woods, gliding in his rowboat over the gently rippled surface of her ponds and rivers. Henry was the personal acquaintance, as friends teased, of every plant and animal that could be found in the area. Accompanied by his older and only brother, John, he climbed trees and hills, waded into ponds and creeks in pursuit of bullfrogs and turtles, lay in the tall grass of an open field watching the clouds tumble past. To accept the confines of four walls and regular hours ran against his grain—perhaps in part because it was expected of him by his straitlaced New England family and neighbors.

When he graduated from Harvard University in the summer of 1837, Thoreau entered a society that offered few opportunities for a young, classically educated idealist with a love of nature. The world had changed dramatically since the turn of the century. The wheels of the industrial revolution had begun to grind, churning out huge factories and warehouses stuffed with mass-produced goods. The steam engine as a means to power transportation had begun to shrink the world, while the nation pushed its boundaries ever westward, leaving worn-out farmland and filthy, overcrowded cities behind. Science was already beginning to butt heads with religion. The country's battle cry was "Progress!"

Henry had two alternatives: become a schoolteacher or join the family pencil-making business. Neither excited him. "I

seek a garret," he mused in the early pages of the journal that was to cover many thousands of pages before his death twenty-five years later. Henry had always been a staunch individualist. Even his physical appearance was unique. Some described him as "strong-featured"; others, such as Mrs. Nathaniel Hawthorne, declared him to be "ugly as sin." A compact man with shortish, sturdy legs, long, wiry arms, and narrow, sloping shoulders, he stood just over five foot seven. His face, with its perpetually ruddy tint from constant exposure to wind and sun and his large, long nose and somewhat receding chin, reminded one friend of a fox. But his eyes were his most memorable feature. They were huge, round, and deep-set beneath thick, expressive brows, appearing blue in some light, gray in others. At times he would seem to be staring, dazed, off into space, a thousand miles away; but he could also fix someone with a pointed glance that seemed to pierce one's inmost thoughts. His generous, drooping mouth, described as "queer" by one acquaintance, often drew into a pout, especially when he did not agree with something, which was a great deal of the time.

As soon as he returned home to Concord from Harvard, he was offered a job at the local academy, Central School, which he felt compelled to accept. He had plenty of innovative ideas about running a classroom. He threw himself wholeheartedly into the new job, as he did most ventures. But after only two weeks, he was taken aside by the school committee and informed that his method of teaching, which involved much field work and hands-on "doing" but little discipline, was far too lax. He was to reinstitute corporal punishment if he wished to keep his post. Tight-lipped and smoldering with indignation, Henry strode back out to the classroom, armed with the hated rod. After administering several whippings in the course of the day, he handed in his resignation. The experience had been too disturbing for him to consider another day's continuance. He could see no possible connection between love of learning and physical pain. A few weeks later, in a letter to a family friend, he reflected that he had come "to regard the cowhide as a nonconductor. Methinks that, unlike the electric wire, not a single spark of truth is ever transmitted through its agency to the slumbering intellect it would address."

Just a few weeks after his commencement ceremony he found himself unemployed and essentially blackballed from the teaching profession. With no work and his brother John teaching in Taunton, time hung heavily on his hands. He was depressed and lonely. In October, he started a journal. "What are you doing now?" his first entry asked, somewhat ruefully. Living in a house full of talkative women who liked to fuss over him, he longed for male companionship, for the good old days of rambling through the woods with John, frequenting special places, and talking of things only his brother could fully understand and appreciate. Although Henry had a lively imagination, he was self-conscious and reserved and given to brooding. John, on the other hand, was easygoing, sunny-natured, and exuberantly spontaneous. With him, Henry was able to let go and show a whimsical, playful side he showed to no one else.

John was without doubt the better-looking of the two. He was, like his brother, below average in height, though somewhat slighter and more elegant in build. He had strong but pleasant features, dark hair, and dark, ever-smiling eyes. Since childhood when they had shared a trundle bed, the two brothers had been inseparable, sharing every thought, possession, and activity. They had even invented a private "pseudo-Indian" language, giving Indian names to various people and places they knew.

The winter of 1837-1838 was long and idle. By March, at the height of cabin-fever season, Henry was restless and sought a sweeping change. He wrote to John, this time to propose that the two of them set off for the wilds of Kentucky and take jobs teaching in one of the new frontier schools. John, always adventurous, immediately agreed and gave his notice at the Taunton school. As the two were packing, Henry received a lead on a job at a school in Alexandria, Virginia. Even though he knew John would be accompanying him out "west," he was beginning to harbor some anxieties about leaving the familiar, gentler landscape of Concord for the tree-shadowed unknown of the frontier. He postponed the trip to pursue this new and safer alternative.

But his trip to Virginia produced no job offer. By the time Henry returned to Concord, John had found another job in Roxbury. Henry was still unemployed and without prospects. He tried a new tack. He had relatives in Bangor, Maine, and felt certain some backwoods school might need a schoolmaster and be beyond the shadow of the Concord blacklist, which had dogged his other efforts. He made a wide circuit on the stagecoach from Portland to Brunswick and Bath, across to Augusta and Gardiner, over to Bangor, and back down to Portland via the coast. Again, no work, and this time because he had arrived a month too late for fall hiring. But the trip proved more fruitful than it seemed at the time. In Old Town, he spent a few hours visiting with an old Indian brave—Governor John Neptune—in whose sharp memory the "old ways" of the forest were still clear and alive. Henry was spellbound and made a promise to himself to return someday to Maine to explore the northern forest and the ways of the red man.

Back in Concord, he decided to open his own private school in the family home and teach in his own way. Although he soon had enough pupils to justify renting the Concord Academy building (a bargain at five dollars a month), he netted only a few dollars for his efforts. But he had nothing else on his horizon, so he held on. With his emphasis on field activities and the practical applications of lessons, Henry's

school began to earn a positive reputation among Concord's intelligentsia. By February 1839, there were enough students to require a second teacher. Henry immediately wrote to John, who was all too happy to leave behind the more structured routine at Roxbury. Together, they embarked on what was to prove the brightest spring and summer of their lives. With John's cheerful influence and no one to answer to, Henry was content to teach school. The students loved both brothers, but found John a warmer, sweeter presence than Henry, whom one pupil described as being "still in the green apple stage."

In their spare time, the Thoreaus took long rambles in the woods, went rowing in their boat *The Rover,* and collected botanical and mineral specimens. John was just as ardent a naturalist as Henry. In the spring, they set to work on a new, improved boat, which they christened *The Musketaquid,* and made plans to take a week off between semesters at the summer's end to cruise up the Concord and Merrimack rivers to the White Mountains of New Hampshire. It wasn't exactly the wilds of Kentucky, but it was to be an adventure all the same.

That summer, shortly before they left on their trip, Ellen Sewall, the sister of one of their prize pupils, came to Concord for a two-week visit and stayed with the Thoreaus, who augmented their income by taking in boarders. She was an amateur naturalist. Dark-haired, blue-eyed, and easy-going, she swept both brothers off their feet. When she returned home to Scituate, both wrote her regularly with high hopes and secret dreams of blossoming romance.

The last week of the month, they loaded their little blue and green vessel with an unwieldy but healthy cargo of melons and potatoes and headed north up the winding waters of the Concord. They talked and laughed, making up names for the new places they encountered, exploring small islands, reveling in their temporary freedom and the miles of unfamiliar, summer-greened scenery that unfolded before them. As the grand finale of the trip, the two climbed to the top of Mount Washington. After spending so many days on the water, the long climb up the rocky mountainside was revitalizing. When at last they stood upon the summit, the unceasing wind whipping about their heads, it was as if they had taken a deep, quenching draught of sky. The huge sweep of unbroken woodlands and the giant hulks of mountains that fanned out before them made Concord seem flat, tame, and tiny. It was an exhilarating moment.

Within a few days, they were back in Concord, where they threw themselves back into their school—and the pursuit of Ellen Sewall. John, ever spontaneous, made an impromptu trip to Scituate to visit her one week while her parents were away. Henry, more self-conscious and cautious, wrote her, enclosing poems and health tips (he urged her to give up coffee and tea). By summer, John had mustered up the cour-

age to ask her to marry him. He traveled back to Scituate and, while walking on the beach, brashly popped the question. She just as brashly accepted; then, under the cloud of her conservative father's disapproval, she changed her mind, much to Henry's relief and delight.

After waiting for a respectable length of time, Henry also tried his luck, in letter form, naturally. He, too, was refused. Sadder and now with a distance between them, however slight, that had never existed before, the brothers settled back into their school routine. It was a stressful winter for John, whose health, undermined by a smoldering case of tuberculosis, was poor. By spring, he was forced to give up his duties at the school. Without him, Henry had little desire to continue and closed their private academy forever.

Once again, he was unemployed. This time, his neighbor, Ralph Waldo Emerson, took pity on him and offered him room and board in exchange for being a handyman-groundskeeper. Henry gratefully accepted. Emerson's household was fertile soil for the still-cautious, uncertain roots Henry was trying to lay down intellectually. The Emerson home possessed an extensive library and was the regular meeting place of the "Hedge Club"—a group of prominent, progressive intellectuals known as "Transcendentalists." Henry soaked up the new ideas with Emerson's encouragement. He began to try his hand at writing poems and essays, several of which Emerson helped to place in the short-lived transcendentalist publication *The Dial.*

Henry's relationship with Emerson was one of the most influential of his life. The industrial revolution and its encouragement of materialism had spurred Emerson and kindred philosophers to examine with vigor the inner spirit of man. Pursuit of the highest ideals and freedom from material attachments were cornerstones of transcendentalist doctrine—concepts compatible with Henry's own ideas. This philosophy confirmed the young schoolteacher in the belief that securing a career merely to earn money and satisfy concerned friends and relatives was hollow folly. Living in harmony with his philosophy of life, however different it was from that of others, was what really mattered. He began to wonder if perhaps his involvement with nature was not merely an idle preoccupation after all, but an ideal occupation.

Just as he was grappling with such concepts, bad news was brought to the Emerson house: John Thoreau was desperately ill and not expected to live. He had cut his finger while stropping his razor on New Year's Day. A nick had, within a week, become severely infected, then progressed into a virulent case of "lockjaw." A doctor had been rushed in from Boston, but the hopeless prognosis was speedily made: death within a day or two. Henry raced home. Day and night he kept vigil at John's bedside. Throughout the entire ordeal, he displayed remarkable, but deceptive, calm.

At first John was lucid and composed. Though in pain and aware that he was facing death, he chatted pleasantly with his brother while consciousness persisted. Then the disease raged toward its merciless climax. Henry was forced to watch as the familiar, kindly face became hideously distorted by agonizing muscle spasms, forced to listen as the once cheerful gentle voice was racked by groans of pain and the mutterings of delirium. And there was nothing he could do. At two o'clock in the afternoon on January 11, 1842, as Henry held him in his arms, John died.

For two weeks, Henry spent most of his time staring into space, dazed and silent. Then his grief erupted violently. He began to display symptoms that mimicked John's. Doctors were called to the bedside, only to conclude there was no apparent physiological reason for his condition. The illness was imagined. The agony, however, was real. After several days, he began to recover. But it was a slow process. For a month, he was confined to the sick chamber and for many weeks after remained debilitated.

The death of his brother represented a crisis that went far beyond the loss of a loved one. Nature, his trusted muse, had with little warning turned on him, exposing her coldest and most unrelenting side. He struggled between reproach and rationalization. "I do not wish to see John ever again—I mean him who is dead," he wrote unconvincingly to his close friend Lucy Brown, Emerson's sister-in-law, on March

2, "but that other whom only he could have wished to see or to be, of whom he was the imperfect representative. . . . "

He tried futilely to make some positive sense out of nature's callousness. On March 11, he reflected in a letter to Emerson, "The wind still roars in the woods as if nothing had happened out of the course of nature. The sound of the waterfall is not interrupted more than if a feather had fallen . . . no genius or virtue so rare and revolutionary appears in town or village, that the pine ceases to exude resin in the wood or beast or bird lay aside its habits. How plain that death is only the phenomenon of the individual or class." He also groped for a meaning in John's death that would somehow elevate him above his despair and give him purpose. "For my part, I could not have done without this experience," he contended to his friend Isaiah Williams in a letter written March 14. "My destiny is now arrived—is now arriving. I believe that what I call my circumstances will be a very true history of myself—for God's works are complete both within and without—and shall I not be content with his success? I welcome my fate because it is not trivial or whimsical. Is there not a soul in circumstances?"

But deep inside, the wound remained open and undressed. For the next several years, he was to be racked by terrifying nightmares on the anniversary of John's death. And never again would he be able to utter his name without a mist of tears in his eyes.

THE PATH TO KATAHDIN

Where'er thou sail'st who sailed with me,
Though now thou climbest loftier mounts,
And fairer rivers dost ascend,
Be thou my Muse, my Brother John.

When he was well enough, Henry returned to the Emersons, who had a special empathy for their young friend: They had lost their five-year-old son Waldo to scarlatina just two weeks after John's death. But even with heartfelt support, Henry did not rally much. In the spring of 1843, Emerson procured a job for him on Staten Island as tutor to his brother William Emerson's children. The consensus among Henry's friends and family members was that the change would do him good.

He took the job, but it proved far from healing. Instead, the contrast—between the Staten Island Emersons, who were rigidly conservative and formal, and his own friends and family back in Concord—filled him with an almost desperate homesickness and made his grief all the more acute. "I have seen such a hollow glazed life as on a painted floor," he confided to his journal. "Such life only as there is in the shells on the mantelpiece." By November he decided to return to Concord permanently. He also resolved to find a quiet, private retreat where he could work through his inner turmoil—and write a book about the trip of *The Musketaquid* in that final shining summer as a personal memorial to John. First, however, there were several old debts to be paid off. He went to work at the pencil factory for several months. In his efforts to minimize work and maximize profits and thereby reduce his obligatory part in the family business, he came up with several innovations that improved the quality of the pencils and increased production.

In addition he worked at a variety of odd jobs to earn the modest amount of money he needed: carpentry, surveying, masonry, yard work—he did a little of everything as long as it didn't keep him away from the woods too long. He still made daily excursions into the country-side—once with disastrous results. On a fishing expedition with friends in the extremely dry spring of 1844, while trying to make a fish chowder in—of all things—a stump, he managed to set the woods on fire. Before it was checked, the blaze had blackened three hundred acres of Concord's prime hardwoods. At first Henry was in a panic of guilt and alarm and ran two miles to get help. Then he threw himself, exhausted and emotionally drained, on a hilltop and watched the billows of smoke and flame roar up the branches of hundreds of trees. He claimed he then decided he had done nothing wrong and felt no more guilt: "I had settled it with myself." If so, perhaps it was because somewhere deep in his still-wounded mind he felt that he and nature were finally even. In any case, it was six years before he could even write about the incident.

Henry sought his sylvan retreat all the more after the fire; in addition to being called a crank, he had now been dubbed "woods burner." The following spring he found the perfect spot at last—a patch of land owned by Emerson on the shores of Walden Pond. He spent three months preparing his new home, a no-frills ten-foot by fifteen-foot cabin, which he constructed himself entirely from scratch. He even cut down the white pines used for the framing. Having often been accused of sponging off his family and being one of the town's foremost loafers (some Concord gossips even believed he disappeared

into the woods each day to drink!), Henry was determined to show the world and himself that he could be completely self-sufficient. He wanted to show that one could live without luxuries in a woodland setting and live well. He also knew he needed to reduce distractions and confront his inner turmoil.

On July 4, 1845, he moved his household belongings (one load in a borrowed cart) out to the cabin and began his novel experiment in living. Away from the distractions of a busy household, he immediately became what we would call today more "centered." His penned words came in torrents. Within less than a year, he had finished the first draft of his book about his trip with John, which he entitled *A Week on the Concord and Merrimack Rivers*, then launched into working on a collection of essays about his life on Walden's shores. By now he had also managed to establish himself as something of a local folk hero among many young intellectuals and he became a popular lecturer.

Inspired by the example set by fellow transcendentalist abolitionists such as Bronson Alcott, Henry had not paid a poll tax in several years as a protest against the government's support of slavery. The local authorities had chosen to indulgently overlook this fact—at least until tax time in the summer of 1846. It could be that the conservative, crusty constable of Concord, Sam Staples, felt that Henry, who had first burned down the woods, then taken to living like a hermit out by the pond and idling his time away, needed to have the reins drawn up short. In any case, in late July Staples arrested him and took him to the local jail. Despite his delight at finally being given a chance to make a statement by being jailed, Henry had been behind bars only a few hours when an anonymous "friend"—probably Aunt Maria Thoreau, who was staying across the street from the jail at her sister's home—slipped over to Sam Staples's house and paid the poll tax for Henry. Staples felt, however, that Henry could use a sobering lesson and let him sit in a jail cell overnight. To Staples's surprise, instead of being properly chastened by the next morning, Henry was enraged that someone had purchased his freedom. Nonetheless, the experience fired him to write an essay that would one day represent a powerful bloodless "shot heard 'round the world": "Civil Disobedience."

Still, something was missing. The wound made by John's death was relieved but not healed. If anything, the void seemed to grow wider as he laid the manuscript of *A Week* aside and faced another summer without his brother's companionship. When his cousin George Thatcher, in Bangor, invited him to come to Maine to accompany him on a trip into the woods, he seized the opportunity. It might be the closest he would ever come to experiencing true wilderness, and he had not lost his deep interest in Indians. It was just the sort of adventure that would have fired John's lively enthusiasm. As plans for the trip progressed, he resolved to climb Mount Katahdin. Few white men had stood upon its broad, wind-hammered summit. Conquering it would be an achievement worthy of a daring adventurer—an achievement worthy of John.

THE FIRST TRIP

Chaos and ancient Night, I come no spy
With purpose to explore or to disturb
The secrets of your realm but . . . as my way
Lies through your spacious empire up to light.

Henry set out for Maine on August 31, 1846—the same day four years before that he had set out up the Concord River for the White Mountains with John. Travelling by steamer from Boston, he reached Bangor the next day. It was a bustling city despite its remote location. The sound of its over two hundred sawmills hummed in a perpetual chorus, and the smell of sawdust hung in the air like strong incense.

After a brief stop at the Thatcher house, Henry and his cousin immediately set out for the Big Woods. In Old Town, they stopped to watch Indian craftsmen building bateaux; Henry took careful notes. He had not lost his fascination for Native American culture. To him, it symbolized the ideal harmony of man with nature, a harmony for which he strove continuously, yet could never quite honestly achieve. This first expedition to Maine was to prove a disappointment with respect to

the Indians, however. In Lincoln, the cousins stopped to hire an Indian guide. The Penobscot Louis Neptune was arranged to join the party at the West Branch Dam. But he never showed up; he went, instead, on a drinking binge. Henry was also dismayed by the living conditions in the Indian community. Most living quarters were abject shacks with a few staid European-style homes and a trim Roman Catholic church. "I even thought that a row of wigwams with a dance of powwows and a prisoner tortured at the stake would be more respectable than this," he complained later in his journal. Despite his vehement feelings on the oppressed conditions of enslaved blacks in the South, his sympathy did not yet extend so generously to the plight of the Indian.

After spending a few nights at "Uncle George" McCauslin's on the West Branch (a day's trip west of Lincoln) and seeing no sign of Neptune, Henry and Thatcher set off for Katahdin by bateau with Mc-Causlin, another acquaintance named Tom Fowler, and two other men. His first taste of wilderness came that night when the party reached the shores of North Twin Lake, which lay well beyond the last homestead in the region. The distant wall of trees confronting him across the dark sheet of water was unsettling. Behind it lay miles of trackless, dense forest where no human being yet dwelled. This was true wilderness. Yet in his journal, he compared the scene, incongruously, to the "civilized aspect" of a distant city. The simile, perhaps, made the prospect seem less alien—and less intimidating.

The next day they crossed Ambajejus Lake, worked their way up the West Branch of the Penobscot River by portaging around the falls, and reached the Sowadunk Deadwater, where their water route ended and their woodland trail to the mountain peak began. After making camp, the men threw their lines into the stream hoping to catch some of the trout for which it was known. Thoreau was astonished at the cascade of fish that was soon tumbling onto the shore at the end of their lines! Speckled trout, with their glinting flecks of gold and rose, white "chivin" with their gleaming silver-white bellies, all "glistened like the fairest flowers, the product of primitive rivers . . . made beautiful, the Lord only knows why, to swim there!" That night, Henry woke up from a dream of trout fishing and seriously wondered if the

"waterfall" of fish had been a part of the same dream. He got up and went to the edge of the water with his fishing rod. As he cast his line into the water, the broad, moon-drenched peak of Katahdin rising into the dark sky beyond, he "found the dream to be real and the fable true."

The next day, they left the bateaux, shouldered their packs, and set out for Katahdin, guided by a compass. Exhausted by ploughing for over eight hours through thick forest threaded only by an occasional, narrow moose trail, they stopped at the mountain's base as the sun's rays began to slant. They made camp next to a roaring mountain stream that seemed to Henry to have erupted from the clouds above. Henry left the group to climb alone while the light held, following the bed of the stream, and scrambling in places over the interlocked crowns of flattened, wind-stunted spruce. When he finally pulled himself up to the treeline, he was confronted by a bleak rubble of gray rock, shadowy and surrealistic in the fading light, a heavy mist pressing down from above. He had the strange sense of being watched in silence by hard, gray eyes. He retreated and climbed back down to the camp to wait for the kinder light of day. That night, the wind pounded the camp like swirling surf, sending sparks from their fire high into the sky, setting a dry spruce ablaze like a torch in some ancient pagan rite. Though exhausted, Henry's excitement kept him awake long into the night.

The next morning dawned sunny and

warm. Immediately after breakfast, the group set out for the mountaintop. Henry was determined to conquer this mountain, to confront its wilderness one on one. He had stuffed everything he brought with him into his pack before he started out with the dim notion that he might have to strike out from the peak alone—why or where to he did not clearly know.

As they ascended, Henry soon left his companions far behind. The day was bright with sunlight, yet as he climbed nearer to the summit, up the rock-strewn slope, a dense mist began to swirl about him, sifting out the sun. The clouds grew denser; the sky appeared only now and then when a blast of wind swept clear a transient pool of blue. At last, he stood near the mountain's summit. Before him stretched an immense, boulder-strewn plain hundreds of acres across, as stark and empty as the moon's face. The clouds and wind boiling around him uneasily, Henry felt dwarfed by the massive, silent landscape. This was not the shining mountaintop he had stood upon four summers before with John when both had been full of life and expectation. This was a barren, forbidding place—vast, savage, and un-

knowable—a place where human ponderings were as insignificant and meaningless as the squeakings of a mouse. Before Henry loomed the raw, unyielding face of nature. It was the face of life—and the face of death. Here on this mountaintop was a god who knew no individual, a nature made from Chaos and Old Night, indifferent to humans. Realization washed over him in a terrifying yet purging wave, and he felt his reason, and with it all anxieties and rationalizations, "dispersed like the air." The mountain seemed to confront him. "Why came ye here before your time?" it seemed to ask. "Should thou freeze or starve or shudder thy life away, here is no shrine, nor altar, nor any access to my ear."

As he stood there, he struggled with the shock of recognition of a different self. He was not an actor on a stage. He was part of the stage itself, as was everything else that he saw, touched, and heard. Within himself lay nature, within himself lay God. "Talk of mysteries!" he later wrote. "Think of our life in nature, daily to be shown matter, to come in contact with it—rocks, trees, wind on our cheeks! The *solid* earth! The *actual* world. The *common* sense. *Contact! Contact! Who* are we? *Where* are we?"

THE SECOND TRIP

Great God, I ask thee for no meaner pelf
Than that I may not disappoint myself

Less than a week later, Thoreau was back in Concord at his cabin on Walden Pond. His conviction in being there had been solidified by his wilderness expedition, while his need to prove anything to anyone—even himself—had diminished.

For the next year, he wrote, lectured, and worked at odd jobs and in his extensive garden at Walden. By the end of the second year at the pond, he had gleaned what he could from the experiment. He was getting restless and, perhaps, a little bored. Two years, two months, and two days after wheeling his belongings through the woods to the cabin at Walden, he loaded them back up and left—for good. For a year he served once more as housekeeper and handyman to the Emersons, while Ralph Waldo was away in England. Then he moved back home with his family. To ensure a more reliable and pleasant means of earning an income than making pencils, he borrowed a compass and chain from Cyrus Hubbard (his own compass

had broken and he could not afford to have it fixed) and went into the surveying business.

Aside from a few brief trips to Cape Cod, New York, and Quebec, Henry was settling into a life deeply rooted in the pastoral soil of Concord. He was also becoming more set in his own way of doing things and therefore considered all the more eccentric by the local standard. He took to wearing an oversized hat that drooped comically over his upper face. He tucked flowers and other botanical specimens he collected under its brim. His thick, wavy, brown hair usually looked "as if it had been dressed by a pine cone" (as one acquaintance described it), and his coat had huge pockets he sometimes sewed himself for storing rocks and other treasures. An old shirt and trousers and worn, unblacked boots with laces that kept coming untied completed his typical outfit. Coming home from his expeditions at night, stems and leaves bristling from under his floppy hat, pockets bulging, he excited many snickers and stares of wonder. The local ladies' auxiliary once even volunteered to make him some new shirts, believing he was simply too hard up to dress more suitably.

His room at home was referred to by family members as "Henry's Den." When the Thoreaus moved at last into a permanent home in 1850, Henry had finally gotten his garret—a finished attic room. The "Den" was a minor source of embarrassment for his fastidious sisters and mother; he refused to allow anyone to disturb his lair or its treasures—even its dust. Animal hides, rocks, birds' eggs, driftwood, thousands of Indian arrowheads, clumps of lichens and moss, dried plants, and armloads of books on flora and fauna filled every available niche. His burgeoning journals took up an entire bookcase. He was content to putter among his treasures by the hour, but he was far from antisocial. He enjoyed family life and came down for an hour or two most evenings to sing, dance alone, play the flute, or entertain the family cat with catnip toys he created himself.

His lectures about his spartan, spiritual woods life, with their humorous observations on the average man's alienation from the natural world, were popular but controversial. He became widely known as "The Hermit of Concord." Many critics condemned the hermit's philosophy as pantheistic and blasphemous, while others dismissed it as merely shallow and selfish. Aunt Maria, never one to mince words,

decried the entire business as "infernal and infernally stupid." Thoreau's increased contact with the public through his lectures, which often took him to larger towns, was leading him to a growing disillusionment with society in general. In most towns larger than Concord, no woods at all remained—just a barren, dirty landscape of stone and clapboard filled with people living "lives of quiet desperation." Greed and hypocrisy, Henry concluded, were the rule rather than the exception.

In 1849, after many revisions and unsuccessful queries to publishers, *A Week on the Concord and Merrimack Rivers* was at last accepted for publication by James Munroe & Company of Boston. His memorial to John would finally be unveiled. But his happiness was disturbed: Just two weeks after the first books came off the press, Henry lost his sister Helen to tuberculosis. Although the book was well reviewed, thanks to the Hedge Club's extensive network of literary contacts, its sales soon went from poor to nonexistent. Munroe & Company began to send him notes asking what they were supposed to do with the six or seven hundred unsold copies. Henry was forced to confront the public failure of his memorial to John. Depression hovered. It was summer again. He was thirty-six years old, considered by many an aging eccentric unable to earn an independent living, one whose finest effort had fallen short. And he was alone.

Once again, he turned to Maine. As soon as he could arrange it—on September

13, 1853—he set out by steamer for Bangor, where he planned to join his cousin George on an excursion into the Maine Woods that would take him deeper into the wilderness than he had ever gone before. Because of the increasing competition from the infant railroad system, steamer fare had dropped from three dollars to one dollar, a bargain appreciated by Henry, who had few dollars to spare. He noticed in the pages of the *Whig and Courier* that even in Maine, rail travel had become popular, with lines now running inland as far as Waterville and Augusta as well as along the coast.

This time, Henry and Thatcher were more fortunate in their choice of an Indian guide. Joe Aitteon, the son of a Penobscot elder, agreed to accompany them. Although only twenty-four, Aitteon was an experienced woodsman, intelligent, and courageous (thirty years later he would drown during a river drive near Millinocket trying to save a crew of men trapped by the falls). But Henry was a little disappointed in Aitteon. He spoke perfect English, dressed like a typical white logger, and occasionally spiced his speech with American slang. He was not the classic red man of Henry's dreams, but he knew the woods, and eventually he won his employer's somewhat grudging respect.

The day after Henry arrived in Maine, he and his cousin set out in a rented wagon for Moosehead Lake, a trip of nearly sixty miles. Thatcher had earlier sent Aitteon ahead to Greenville on Moosehead's southern shore. It rained all day and was still pouring so heavily by late afternoon that they were forced to hold over for one night in Monson, fifteen miles south of Moosehead, at Fogg's public house on Lake Hebron. The next morning at sunrise, they connected with Aitteon in Greenville and took the steamer up to the Northeast Carry at the head of the lake, nearly forty miles to the north. Their fellow passengers included hunters, loggers, cows, and sheep. The carry was a short, crude railroad that connected Moosehead with the Penobscot River and consisted of a few open cars pulled by oxen over a log rail. After a slow, uncomfortable journey of about two miles, they launched their birchbark canoe, loaded down almost to the waterline with supplies, at the Penobscot's upper West Branch.

Thatcher and Aitteon were both enthusiastic hunters and wasted no time getting down to business. Their quarry was moose. Moose and caribou, not deer, were the dominant species of the great northern forest at that time, although caribou were becoming scarce in settled areas. On the first night, after making camp and waiting for darkness to fall, the two hunters drifted silently along the river in their canoe, stalking any moose that might venture down to the water in search of small water plants. Though he was not a hunter, Henry tagged along. They did not see any moose, but Henry was enchanted by the scene. Above the silent, glinting, onyx water, the silhouettes of the evergreens rose like steeples against the star-sprinkled sky. Before they crawled under their blankets to sleep, they heaped armloads of logs on their campfire, a pit some four feet deep by ten feet long, which sent streamers of sparks high above the treetops, and consumed enough firewood, as Henry observed, to "last a poor family in one of our cities all winter."

The next day, they floated down the river along the wide, sluggish stretch known as the Pine Stream Deadwater. As they drifted past a meadow, Henry's alert ears caught the sound of branches snapping. He called Aitteon's attention to the alder thicket they'd just passed. Joe paddled back to the spot in time for the two of them to catch a glimpse of a cow moose with her calf peering at them through the alders. From where he sat, Thatcher could not even tell for certain what kind of animal was there, but he stood up in the canoe and fired a shot over his companions' heads. The cow dashed up the bank to the edge of the deeper woods. Its calf, confused, broke into the open water, bleating pitifully, its dark-ringed eyes wide as its mother watched from the shadow of the woods. Thatcher shot at the calf, which froze in alarm. Then it, too, ran for the shelter of the forest where the deep carpet of pine needles and moss betrayed no sound.

On shore, Aitteon found the cow's tracks and traces of blood and followed them. When he gave up after less than half an hour, Henry was somewhat disillu-

sioned with the Indian's hunting prowess. A half hour after Thatcher had fired his shot, they were headed back down the river. They put ashore to make a carry; Aitteon had not walked far when he came upon the cow's body. Henry's initial rush of excitement and curiosity drowned out all other emotions. He was at last to get an opportunity to see this living myth of Maine up close. He quickly created a makeshift tape measure out of the canoe's painter and set to work measuring every part of the immense, still-warm body. Then, as he stood aside to let Aitteon begin the work of skinning the beast, his excitement gave way to remorse. As the Indian slit the gut from sternum to tail, the milk from the cow's udder mingled with her blood. Henry recalled the "frightened rabbit" look and plaintive cry of the now-orphaned calf.

Aitteon took the hide, a large mass of meat, and the tongue and nose (a traditional Abenaki delicacy) and left the rest of the carcass. Then he and Thatcher, followed reluctantly by Henry, traced fresh moose tracks up the trail, hoping for another kill. Thatcher, whom Henry derisively referred to as "our nimrod" in his journal, shot at everything that moved, it seemed. But all he bagged during the afternoon was a porcupine he'd mistaken for a bear.

That night the party, including Henry, feasted on moose meat, which Henry described as flavorful. Then Aitteon and Thatcher set off once more under cover of darkness. Henry stayed behind at the camp. Late into the night, he sat brooding by the fire, listening to the night birds and the rustle of leaves. As he stared out at the shadowy shapes of the trees, his stomach stuffed with moose meat, the forest seemed to crowd around him accusingly. It was he who had betrayed the moose's hiding place, he who had stood by and watched a pointless killing. He was no better than the hunters he held in contempt, his soul no more free from hypocrisy; and through his part in the afternoon's tragedy he had proved himself just as alienated from nature. It was to be many weeks before the shadow of guilt and self-disgust would leave his mind.

The next day the party headed out to Chesuncook Lake. For a distance of nearly half a mile as they paddled north, Henry could see behind them the red, wasted carcass of the moose still lying in silent accusation on the riverbank. That night they arrived at the forest farm of Ansell Smith on the southern shore of Chesuncook. Smith's cabin had been built only a few years before. It was crude and rough, but the farm was self-sufficient. Unlike Henry's cabin at Walden, there was no town to walk to daily for supplies or company, no mother and sisters to deliver hot pies and cakes every Sunday afternoon. This was a true survival homestead. Henry was filled with admiration for the place even though it made Walden appear somewhat artificial.

Smith's farm was a regular stopover for loggers headed into the forest around Chesuncook, which had been opened up to logging just a decade or so before. With their axes, oxen, and little else, loggers had set out like hungry hunters, hot on the trail of the white pine. When Thoreau talked to them, few spoke of the ancient pine's beauty and grandeur. Instead, their conquests were framed in terms of how many oxen could stand on the stump of a fallen tree, of whether or not the trunk was straight and rot-free enough to produce much good wood, and of where the trees easiest to get could be found. As far as Henry was concerned, it was just another form of murder, and the lumber and clapboards that went to create the homes of Concord and countless other towns and cities were little better than the spoils of a devastating war—a war against the forest. Already, he learned, most of the good stands of white pine had been cut: The "enemy" was in retreat.

After leaving Smith's, the party returned up the Penobscot. They spent their last night in the wilderness at an Indian camp. Although Henry had the option to go instead to a nearby logger's cabin, the Indians' encampment, for all its dirtiness, seemed the purer alternative. The Indians were smoking moose meat and hides using the ancient method. Little of their kill was wasted—even the blackened, soiled globs of meat that littered the ground around the fire were saved. Henry lay awake for a long time, eyes closed, listening to them talk in their native Abenaki tongue. Through the sound, he tried to imagine the world into which their roots still stretched deep in time, the world before the coming of the white man. In his dreams, he could see the misty shapes of cougar, caribou, and wolves threading their way through the cool, silent, green shadows of the ancient forest, pursued by red men with slender bows of white ash.

When he awoke, a cold rain was falling.

*T*HE LAST TRIP

Long enough I had heard of irrelevant things; now at length I was glad to make acquaintance with the light that dwells in rotten wood.

When Henry returned to Concord, he was ready to face the unsold copies of *The Week,* which soon arrived. He carried them upstairs to his attic lair. "I have now a library of nearly nine hundred volumes, over seven hundred of which I wrote myself," he dryly commented to a friend. But his conviction concerning the worth of the book and the validity of his own unique perspective on life and nature had become stronger. After Christmas, he launched into a seventh revision of *Walden,* which he had been grinding and polishing for over half a decade. In March he took it to Ticknor and Fields, who immediately offered to publish it—and on exceptionally good terms.

When *Walden* arrived at the bookstores, it created a sensation. For half a year, Henry was the center of literary controversy and attention. Reviewers lauded and lampooned him with equal enthusiasm. Lecture offers poured in. Intellectuals and lost souls made pilgrimages to Concord to meet him. The year 1854 was the pinnacle of his career, which was, like his final summer with John, all too quickly to fade into the mists. By the summer of 1855, the lecture offers had all but dried up as well as much of the other expressions of interest in the Hermit of Concord. Henry began to descend into an emotional valley. He toyed with the idea of retreating to Maine again, this time for a late-winter expedition. But in March 1856, his health suddenly failed. In a strange manifestation of his incipient tuberculosis or perhaps as a symptom of stress, his legs became weak, almost useless, for several months. His long walks and his surveying business came to an end. He was depressed, lonely, and withdrawn.

In July 1856, he took a trip to Cape Cod, hoping the sea air would prove revitalizing. The rest and break from Concord restored his energy and temporarily coaxed back to life his spark of humor and optimism. His essays written on this trip, later collected into a book published after his death, are among his lightest works. Back in Concord, he settled into his familiar routine of writing and ranging the woods and fields. His growing loneliness spurred him to accept more invitations to visit friends who lived beyond Concord, though he never stayed anywhere longer than a few days. He was also becoming more absorbed by the miseries of the oppressed, and donated whatever help his limited finances—and limited time—could provide to blacks seeking escape from slavery via the Underground Railroad, which ran through Concord. He also became a trusted friend to the Irish immigrants in the region who, having escaped the horror of the potato famine in the "Old Country," were now being unscrupulously exploited by their employers.

In the summer of 1857, Henry turned forty. He felt success had come and gone and left him no more content or fulfilled than he had been at twenty or twenty-five. He was still alone and still struggling to achieve an inner harmony with an outer world that seemingly had no real place for him or his ideas. He had come to have a more functional and less romantic relationship with nature; perhaps he had accepted the fact that he could never break free and live entirely on her terms. Yet through his simple, nonconsuming lifestyle, he struggled to keep the bridge between nature and himself open. Although his lecture audiences often accused him of

urging a "return to the savage state," Henry knew society had gone too far to reverse direction. Yet his inner conflict was often acute, his sense of personal failure always a demon lurking just below the surface.

A week after his fortieth birthday, he returned to Maine for what was to prove his final trip. This time he took only one white companion, young Edward Hoar. Hoar had travelled once already to California and possessed the sense of adventure and stamina Henry sought in a travelling companion. On July 20, the two set out. Because he had been seasick throughout both of his other two Boston-to-Bangor steamer voyages, Henry decided to take the train as far as Portland, then board the ship. Much to his chagrin, instead of spending less time in discomfort, a heavy fog kept the steamer at sea even longer than the usual Boston-to-Bangor run.

The two travellers reached George Thatcher's home in time for tea on the twenty-first. They spent a pleasant evening catching up on family news. While there, Henry glanced through the latest issue of the *Whig and Courier*. He was astounded to find that nearly an entire page was taken up by advertisements for clippers, trains, and steamers—all headed west. The advertisement for the stagecoach headed into the Maine Woods was by comparison a tiny patch of print.

The next morning, Thatcher drove Henry up to Old Town to find a guide. When they arrived at Indian Island, it was nearly deserted. An outbreak of smallpox had caused a panicked exodus out of the area. The nightmare of the lethal plagues that had ravaged the tribe over a century before was still burned like a brand into the memory of most. The island was eerily quiet under a heavily overcast sky as Henry and Thatcher walked up the path from the shore past the small, trim Catholic church. Not far from the ferry landing, in the yard of a gracious New England saltbox, they came upon a tall, powerfully built man scraping a deer hide draped over a log. When he turned to greet them, Henry saw that the man, who was in his late forties, had a broad face and strong features, with deepset, unfathomable black eyes and a deep russet complexion. Thatcher knew the man well and introduced him to Henry. His name was Joe Polis. When Thatcher asked him if he knew of any Indian who would be interested in guiding an expedition into the Maine Woods, Polis replied, "Me like to go myself. Me want to get some moose."

Then, with a twinkle in his eye, he asked Thatcher what had become of the last Indian guide he'd taken to the woods: No one had seen or heard from him since. They dickered over price. Polis, who needed money just then, asked for two dollars a day plus a few dollars for the use of his canoe. But when he found that Henry could not pay that price, he relented and agreed to go for one dollar and fifty cents per day with fifty cents per week for the canoe. As they left the island, Thatcher told Henry how lucky he'd been to secure Polis,

who was a member of the Indian "aristocracy" and one of the most reputable and steady guides he knew. That evening, Polis arrived in Bangor on the train with his canoe. Henry met him and led the way to Thatcher's house, nearly a mile away, while Polis followed with the canoe on his head. Frustrated by the Indian's lack of responsiveness when he tried to initiate friendly conversation, Henry wrote in his journal, "In answer to the various observations which I made by way of breaking the ice, he only grunted vaguely from beneath his canoe once or twice so I knew he was there."

The next morning, Henry, Hoar, and Polis caught the stage together to Moosehead. They lashed the canoe to the top—a routine piece of luggage for this stage. The two Massachusetts men were loaded down with gear: hard bread, pork, coffee, rubber shoes and capes, a tent, frying pans, pots, and utensils. Henry was impressed and a little embarrassed to see that all that Polis had brought with him was an axe and a blanket, along with a new pipe and a full pouch of tobacco. At the Bangor House, four hunters climbed into the coach. They had a small arsenal of rifles and ammunition and a hunting dog, which they forced to run alongside the stage. After three miles, the exhausted dog dropped out of sight. Much to Henry's irritation, the owner insisted that the coach stop while he went in search of his pet. What seemed to Henry like eons later, the hapless animal was brought back and tied to the top of the coach in the rain that had just begun to fall, a rope around its neck. On more than one occasion, the beast fell off and dangled outside the coach window until it was rescued.

Throughout the hunters' endless conversation concerning dogs and hunting, the Indian sat in silence on the front seat. If anyone spoke to him, his replies were brief and vague, making him seem stolid and dull-witted. Nonetheless, Henry was angered by the tone some of the whites used in addressing his guide, as if he were a child or an idiot. At such times Polis's dark eyes would subtly flash, yet he would say nothing, or merely grunt in reply. At a tavern, a drunk asked to "borrow" his pipe. Polis, without even looking at him, said he had no pipe, though Henry had seen it only a short time before. Henry was beginning to understand that the stony silence and unresponsiveness of the Indian was simply a defense—little different, as he put it later, from the "*conventional* palaver" that formed the smoke screen of the white man. As they travelled along the road, gray and uninteresting in the rain, Polis handed Henry a copy of *Gleason's Pictorial* he'd picked up along the way. On the cover was a melodramatic sketch of a stagecoach in Washington County, Maine, being pursued by a pack of fierce wolves. Henry read through the accompanying article with intense interest, eyes growing ever wider as it detailed the story of the stage and its alleged frequent attacks by wolves. He glanced up to see that Polis had been watching him with a vague gleam of amusement in his eyes. The story proved to be fabricated.

They reached Moosehead at nightfall. When they stepped off the coach, the air was filled with the raucous chorus of frogs along the shore, something Henry hadn't heard since spring, back in Concord. At dawn the next day, they launched their canoe. As they paddled along, Henry asked Polis the Indian names of every bird and plant they encountered. Polis patiently told him, repeating each until Henry had memorized them or written them out phonetically. When Henry later asked if he would be able to reside on Indian Island to learn the Abenaki language, Polis said yes, it was possible. When asked how long he thought it would take, Polis dryly estimated that Henry's schooling would probably last one week, whereupon Henry just as dryly replied that in that case, while on their trip, Polis could teach him everything he knew.

They soon came within sight of Mount Kineo looming above a peninsula that jutted out into the lake. It was a gigantic mass of rock with sheer cliffs of nearly eight hundred feet that seemed to erupt from the gleaming surface of the water. Polis told them, with much aplomb, an Indian legend concerning the mountain. Kineo, so the story went, had once been a giant cow moose, which was one day slain by a great Indian brave. Her calf had escaped but was later killed to the southeast among the islands of the Penobscot Bay. To the Indians, the island looked from certain angles like a fallen moose. Polis, who may have heard Joe Aitteon recount the story of Thatcher's moose hunt of four years before, asked with pretended wonder how the great hunter might have killed such a mighty moose. Sensing he was being ribbed, Henry was rankled. He later tersely commented in his journal that the Indian's moose tale had been just a second-rate story—poorly made up for by a "drawling tone, long-windedness, and a dumb wonder which he [Polis] hopes will be contagious."

They made camp on Kineo in a dense spruce thicket. After lunch, Hoar and Henry climbed to the top of the mountain. The rain clouds were still churning above the lake, but from that "glorious wild view," which encompassed three hundred sixty degrees of forest, lake, and sky, they could see signs of clearing to the north, while to the south, murky clouds trailing wreaths of rain hovered just above the mountains. Henry was exhilarated to witness the changing weather from such a perspective. On the way down, they met Polis coming up. He had been fishing on the lake for their supper while they explored. He was surprisingly winded from the climb, prompting Henry to comment in his journal that "perhaps he believed he was climbing over the back of a tremendous moose." Later that night, as the campfire crackled in the black shadows of the spruce, Polis sang them a Jesuit-taught religious hymn in the Abenaki language, his voice piercing the still night air with its

"nasal yet musical chant." Henry was moved by the honest and unaffected faith it expressed. There was nothing "dark and savage" in this faith or about the Indian. "There was indeed a beautiful simplicity about it," Henry wrote in his journal.

Sometime after midnight Henry woke, chilled, and rose to replenish the fire. There, among the smoldering ashes, he discovered a strange, glowing, white ring of light. He traced the source to phosphorus in a chunk of rotting moosewood. He was so excited by the phenomenon that he woke Hoar to share it with him. Never before had he seen such a wonderful light. With his pocket knife, he cut out chips of the glowing material and held them in his hand. His fingers and palm began to glow as if with an inner light. Despite years spent investigating every detail of the woods, he had never encountered this magical material. "I let science slide and rejoiced in that light as if it had been a fellow creature," he later wrote. "I believed that the woods were not tenantless but choked full of honest spirits . . . not an empty chamber in which chemistry was left to work alone. . . ." A surge of hope and romance filled his soul. The whole world once again seemed new and full of wonder. What real meaning did science and its endless classification have in the face of an experience like this, he asked himself. It was only the subjective, not objective, experience that in the end had any real and enduring meaning. Here in the wilderness, undisturbed by humans, nature was still free to weave an unbroken spell of wonder, to flow like a bright, renewing fountain.

The next day he learned that Polis was very familiar with the phenomenon of "fox fire." He had seen it many times, as had all his people. For them, such magic was an accepted part of everyday life. This revelation renewed Henry's appreciation for the red man. They had, after all, lived for many years in this forest day and night, spring through winter. "Nature must have made a thousand revelations to them which are still secrets to us," he marveled. This experience reaffirmed for him how much more could be learned through long, patient observation of undisturbed nature in her own domain than from any scientist poring over dusty books and old specimens in a laboratory!

He was coming to see that Polis's "vagueness," which had earlier irritated him, did not reflect slowness or a lack of precise knowledge. Rather, Indians lived more in the moment, and relied on a different level of intelligence than the white man's. "Not having experienced the need of the [white man's] sort of knowledge, all labeled and arranged, he has not acquired it." Henry concluded that the Indian's knowledge, especially of nature, was far more immediate, fluid, and useful. "I rejoice to find that intelligence flows in other channels than I knew," he wrote. "It redeems for me portions of what seemed brutish before."

The next day they reached Northeast Carry and before dark had made it a few miles down the Penobscot River, heading north, before stopping to make camp. The day after was Sunday. Polis announced he did not wish to travel on the Sabbath and proposed that they lay over for the day. When pressed by Hoar and Henry, who were far too eager to sit around for twenty-four hours, he relented and said it would perhaps be acceptable to work if he did not take any pay. Henry was later amused to see that he had nonetheless not deducted any pay from his final bill. By the next day, they were crossing the Umbazooksus, a small lake at the head of the Caucomgomoc River. As they paddled along, Polis accidentally spit on Henry's back. He wiped it off and told the lonely bachelor it was a sign he would soon be married. At the next portage, Polis, who was very familiar with the route, went on ahead with the canoe and told his two companions to follow in the trail he would leave in the mud. They started out with Hoar insisting on making two trips for every distance they covered in order to transport their supplies more easily. After a few miles, it became apparent that they had taken the wrong trail. As Henry sat waiting for Hoar to return with his pack, the blackflies, still thick despite the lateness of the season, began to harass him. He was relieved to remember that Mrs. Thatcher had made up an insect repellent and tucked it in his pack. It worked fairly well, but the concoction, a mixture of spearmint, camphor, turpentine, and sweet oil, proved to be almost as distasteful as the blackflies.

When Hoar returned on his last trip, Polis was with him. The Indian had back-tracked, then traced their likely path through the woods. They were now so far off course that Polis decided the best plan was for him to return to the canoe and bring it up to Chamberlain Lake while Hoar and Henry pressed, by compass, through the swamp before them to the lake. This became the most miserable walk of Henry's life. Every step they took sank them up to their knees in black, oozing mud or soggy moss well sprinkled with moose droppings, "a mossy and moosey swamp." Fallen, rotted trees lay in their path, forming an obstacle course. Nowhere was there a dry place to sit down. The thick spruce and cedar canopy enveloped the swamp in perpetual gloom; the blackflies and mosquitoes swirled around them like clouds while moose flies swarmed about their faces. When they finally broke out of the swamp on the open shore of Chamberlain Lake, they plunged into the water up to their waists to wash away the noxious black slime. They were too tired that night to bother pitching their tent. They ate dinner, then stretched out on the pebbly beach with their blankets. But sleep was fitful. The dry sand was the domain of the "no-see-um," a tiny sand fly worse than the blackflies they had escaped. But Henry felt somewhat compensated for his misery. He heard, deep in the night, the eerie, quavering laughter of a loon—the very voice of the wilderness for him.

The next morning, after rinsing out their clothing and drying it in the sun, the party set off north across Chamberlain Lake, the largest of the Allagash lakes. Henry saw that the entire shoreline was ringed by a stark barrier of dead trees. They had been killed when the lake's level had been raised by the logging company dam built at its outlet. Bleached by the sun and water, the gnarled, twisted roots, trunks, and branches looked like chaotic piles of huge bones. Henry was angered to think that such wholesale destruction had been caused just to float the choicest pines out of the forest. "Think how much land they have flowed without asking nature's leave!" he mused in his journal. After passing through the northern outlet of Chamberlain, they were at last on the Allagash River, which Polis had told them meant "hemlock bark" in the Abenaki language. Two miles up, they came to Heron Lake (now Eagle Lake). Henry noticed that its shores were "in the same ragged and unsightly condition" as Chamberlain's. They put ashore on a small island. There Henry found several new plant specimens for his collection. Polis told him the Indian name of each as well as the medicinal use according to Indian tradition. The Indian remarked, as they walked along the driftwood-choked shore, that the Heron Lake area had once been home to large numbers of caribou. The sight of the dead trees left by the dam had, according to Polis, driven them away: "No likum stump—when he see that, he scared."

During the afternoon, a thunderstorm

suddenly blew in from the west. The three pitched the tent in record time and climbed into it with their baggage just as the deluge broke. The sky was a strange, angry hue, like a huge, spreading bruise. Thunder—the "grandest" Henry had ever heard—boomed across the lake, echoing off the surrounding mountains like cannon fire. Even Polis, who had experienced many a wilderness storm, was impressed: "It must be good powder!" he quipped. As soon as there was a letup in the storm, the men packed up their gear and set out across the lake, hoping to reach the more sheltered area of the dam before another "salvo" was released. They had barely made it to the outlet and put ashore when the storm picked up again. Polis dived under the canoe while Hoar and Henry huddled beneath the lip of the wooden dam. In the face of such an assault by nature, even Henry, who had been terrified of thunderstorms as a child, admitted they were "more scared than wet."

Just before sunset, with yet another storm chasing them, they headed out onto Chamberlain Lake for Chamberlain Farm, a homestead similar to Ansell Smith's on Chesuncook, on the north side of the big lake. The wind and waves were building and daylight rapidly failing when they made it to the safety of the farm's cleared shores. While Polis and Hoar pitched the tent, Henry ran up to the large log farmhouse to buy some sugar. In just a week, Polis, who dumped almost half a cup of sugar into every dipper of tea he drank, had

almost singlehandedly consumed six pounds! But the Indian had brought them safely thus far, and, especially in the wake of the afternoon's adventures, Henry did not begrudge paying twenty cents a pound for the brown sugar the farm had on hand.

They set out before breakfast the next day, headed southeast for the East Branch of the Penobscot, which would take them back toward Bangor through the wildest possible country. Before midday, they had crossed Chamberlain and Telos, a small lake just beyond Chamberlain's easternmost outlet, and were making their way down Webster Stream toward Grand Lake, which emptied into the Penobscot. Webster Stream was shallow, rocky, and swift-moving—not for novice canoeists. So Henry and Hoar shouldered some of the baggage and did most of the fifteen-mile trip on foot while Polis shot the rapids alone. Late that afternoon, they came upon a large burned-over area. The exposed and eroded hillocks along the stream reminded Henry of "great rock waves," broken only by the charred shells and stumps of dead trees. As they passed over this stark terrain, Henry left Hoar briefly to help Polis pull the canoe over a short rocky fall. When he returned, Hoar had disappeared!

Henry and Polis searched the entire area until nightfall, their vain shouts drowned by the roar of the stream. But Hoar seemed to have been swallowed up. All night long Henry brooded. Surrounded by the lifeless, moon-shadowed landscape of the burned land, he felt isolated and afraid. He was once again forced to confront his own ineffectual tininess before the enormity of the wilderness. A human being lost in this sea of trees was even more insignificant than the proverbial needle in a haystack. Henry was again struck by the red man's superiority in the forest. He and Hoar, without a well-marked trail or a compass, were helpless, while Polis could find his way between any two points in the wilderness relying on only his own less structured but more attuned perceptions. How could they find Hoar if he had stumbled too far afield? What would Henry tell his family? Wrenched by such thoughts, he finally fell into a fitful sleep.

The next morning they made a short portage to the East Branch, the easiest route to Grand Lake, to which they suspected Hoar might have proceeded. Henry had forced Polis to press on without breakfast, although the Indian seemed to have increasingly little patience with the situation. Only a white man such as Hoar, who considered himself a good woodsman, could have gotten himself so inconveniently lost. They had gone only a mile or so when they heard Hoar call to them from just around the next bend. In a burst of relief, Henry shouted again and again in reply. Polis merely snapped, "He hears you!"

Early in the afternoon they reached the lake. At the outlet, Polis spied and shot a cow moose. Henry did not stay to watch the skinning this time. He went fishing. Polis, they learned, depended on moose

hides for most of his income. Under ordinary circumstances, he would also have dried the meat, leaving only the bones behind, but since he was in the pay of Henry and Hoar, he did not bother. Nonetheless, he loaded the hide and nearly a hundred pounds of meat into the canoe.

They camped that night on the lakeshore, where Polis made them some checkerberry tea. The next day, they proceeded down the East Branch. It was a veritable wild staircase of falls and carries at that time of year, made somewhat more tolerable for Henry by the abundance of ripe blueberries and raspberries that grew along the rocky shore. At one carry, Polis pointed out a caribou's track. When they returned to get the rest of their gear, the Indian discovered a new, even rarer track, that of a mountain lion, near the caribou's. As they prepared to carry around a falls, Polis challenged Henry to a foot race. As a handicap, Polis would take the canoe while Henry would carry the remaining, lighter gear. At first, Henry shot by Polis, but then had to stop as frying pans, spoons, and dippers went flying. As he gathered them up, Polis overtook him, only to have Henry rally and pass him at a run, clutching a blanket filled with pots and pans under one arm and a sooty kettle under the other. When Polis, panting and puffing, finally caught up to him, he was laughing merrily. "Oh, me love to play sometimes!" Once so disillusioned with the Indians, Henry now found himself flattered to have won the respect of Polis, though his only "trophy" was a permanent streak of soot from the kettle on his brown linen shirt.

That night the Indian came down with a severe case of what Henry suspected to be colic. The next day they bought Polis some brandy in Lincoln, a village forty miles north of Old Town. It did no good, and he refused to take any pills from the local white apothecary. He finally prepared his own "medicine": a few teaspoons of black powder mixed in water—an old Abenaki remedy. By morning he had recovered.

That day they stopped just south of the mouth of the Passadumkeag River to eat. Polis told them that in "old times," Indians used to stop near there to dig red ochre used for ceremonial makeup. Just before reaching Old Town, the Indian decided to give Henry a lesson in the Abenaki method of paddling—an offer Henry knew to be a gesture of respect and acceptance. After travelling forty miles in less than a full day, they arrived at Indian Island. Polis offered to sell them his canoe, but after financing the trip—which included an extra ten pounds of premium-priced sugar!—Henry had no cash to spare. He left Polis at his big white house and headed for the train to Bangor. It was the last he would see of the Indian.

GREEN SHADOWS

Go thou my incense upward from this hearth,
And ask the gods to pardon this clear flame.

Two months after Henry returned from Maine, his father was stricken with jaundice. Although the elder Thoreau survived, his health was ruined. Henry was forced to assume most of the duties of head of household, including more involvement with the pencil business. That fall Emerson helped persuade Henry to submit an essay to the fledgling magazine *The Atlantic Monthly.* In May of 1858, the first installment of "Chesuncook," detailing his second trip to Maine, was published. Henry was pleased—until the second installment appeared. Without his permission, the editor, James Russell Lowell, had deleted a sentence paying tribute to the white pine: "It is as immortal as I am, perchance to go to as high a heaven, there to tower above me still." Lowell thought the idea of a tree possessing a soul was blasphemy and might offend too many readers. Henry was outraged. He refused to submit another article to the *Atlantic* until after Lowell was no longer editor, despite

the fact that it paid more for his stories than any other publication.

Despite his added family responsibilities, Henry still found time to take his daily hikes and perform his own private studies of nature. The latter included such exercises as standing in a swamp for several hours at a time to observe the habits of the bullfrog, or measuring every snowdrift in an area to establish the pattern of drift. During his quiet hours, he worked alone in his den compiling a reference book on the American Indian, a project fired all the more by his contact with Joe Polis. He made regular entries to his ever-expanding journal and worked at pulling into essay form his observations on patterns of forest growth—observations that reading Charles Darwin's newly published book *The Origin of Species* helped to crystallize.

In February 1859, John Thoreau, Sr., died. The strain of his new responsibilities had already begun to tell on Henry. His health seemed tied to the seasons. In winter, his chronic cough was worse, and he became increasingly sensitive to cold. In spring and summer, with increased fresh air and exercise, he improved. But the overall trend was downward.

A few months after Henry's father died, the obsessed and charismatic abolitionist John Brown came to Concord to drum up support for his "freedom fighters" in the Kansas territory. Henry attended one of his lectures and was profoundly moved. Here at last was a man willing to pay more than mere lip service to his ideals, one who was ready to lay down his life for what he knew to be right. Henry had become ever more disgusted with the armchair altruism he encountered daily and the blindness most people had toward the roots of evil growing right beneath their own feet. Brown immediately became his idol. After Brown was arrested for his famous raid on Harper's Ferry in 1859, Henry wrote one of the most impassioned speeches of his life: "A Plea for Captain John Brown."

In the fall of 1860, Henry read his completed essay "The Succession of Forest Trees" before the Middlesex Agricultural Society. He had, over the years, discovered that reforestation occurred in distinct, successive stages of growth and that each successive, colonizing species of tree was dependent on the one that came before it. His observations struck a chord of truth, and the farmers attending the lecture applauded him enthusiastically. By that winter, Henry's health had plummeted. His

cough was constant, and he began to lose weight steadily. When he was well enough to travel the following spring, he set off by train for an extended trip to Minnesota. The dry, clean air of the plains was believed to benefit "consumptive" patients. He was too weak to do more than admire the new scenery unfolding before him from the train, and once he got to the "Land of a Thousand Lakes," he could take only short hikes in quest of new plant specimens for his collection back home. On a side trip to Redwood Falls, Minnesota, he had the chance to watch a large group of Sioux Indians perform a ceremonial dance. It proved the high point of a draining and unproductive trip.

By late fall he was virtually housebound, too weak to hike farther than the post office. Still, he continued to write, sometimes with his sister Sophia's assistance. *The Atlantic Monthly,* now owned by Ticknor and Fields, had a new editor, James Pierce. He eagerly solicited articles from Henry, who willingly obliged now that Lowell was gone. Ticknor and Fields also decided to reissue *Walden.* Henry was pleased, but asked in April if they would also consider reissuing *A Week on the Concord and Merrimack Rivers.* Fields, sensing somehow the special importance that the book had to the dying author, came to Concord only a week later and bought every remaining unsold copy of Henry's memorial to John. Through the winter and spring, until he became too weak to write at all, Henry worked intermittently on putting into book form his journal entries and essays concerning his final trip to Maine. He never completed the work and cryptically observed that it was "in a knot I can never untie." (Sophia edited the work, and it was published in 1864.)

His thoughts, as he felt death daily growing closer, wandered back to Maine and the wilderness, like a river to its remote source. Whenever he had felt most in conflict, weak, and alone, he had turned to the forest. There he had found true strength and freedom, and had been given back his perspective. Within its healing green shadows he had gained release from pain, reaffirmation of life, and renewal. How he yearned for those green shadows now! On the morning of May 6, 1862, as he sank quietly back on his pillow on the narrow rattan bed he had used at the cabin in Walden and as the light in his gray-blue eyes faded, his mind travelled back to the wilderness. The last sentence he uttered contained only two clearly heard words: "moose" and "Indian."

PART THREE

The Maine Woods Today

KINGDOM OF LOGS: THE MAINE WOODS TODAY

For a man is rich in proportion to the number of things which he can afford to let alone.

When Henry David Thoreau lay dying in 1862, the "endless wilderness" of Maine was rapidly beginning to disappear. The pine, now scarce in many regions, had been supplanted by spruce in importance to loggers. The last wolf had been seen in the southern half of the state and was now rare even in the north.

Nationally, to finance the Civil War, the government had begun to auction off federal lands, which included most remaining wildlands, for as little as pennies per acre. The Swamp Lands Act of 1850 spelled doom for the millions of acres of wetlands that were drained, while the Homestead Act (1862) gave millions of unexploited acres away to settlers. Few settlers headed for the wilderness frontier of Maine, however. The strong economy and convenience of the state's coastal regions and the

frontier lands out West made homesteading in inland Maine—with its bitter winters, dense forest, and isolation—relatively unattractive. However, the vast network of streams and rivers that wove through the forest and drained into busy seaports made the Maine Woods a logger's dream. Millions of board feet of timber were readily accessible to axmen, sawmills, and ships bound for markets in other states and overseas.

As early as the mid-1700s, speculators from other regions, such as David Pingree of Massachusetts, began to buy up huge tracts of forestland for a song, with an eye to logging. And as roads were blazed ever farther northward, logging flourished. For over a century, no state in the Union could touch Maine in lumber production. In the economic long-run—at least for the privileged few who possessed it—the land had far more value as a source of timber, cut or standing, than it did as potential acreage for hardscrabble farms. Thus was born the tradition, still alive and tenacious, of the private ownership of the Maine Woods. Today, ninety-six percent of the Pine Tree State—the highest percentage of any state in the United States—is privately owned.

So while Ohio and Kentucky were being opened to homesteaders, the Maine forest was becoming the kingdom of "logger barons" who loosed thousands of teams of choppers, oxen, and horses into the deepest green recesses. Still cutting only with axes (the big crosscut saws associated with "old-time" logging did not come into universal use until the 1880s), loggers were able to remove over two hundred million board feet of lumber from the Maine Woods each year in the 1850s. Within a few decades, all the best accessible trees, both pine and spruce, had been stripped from the northeastern states. Many logging companies, interested only in the highest return for the smallest possible investment, headed west in search of cheaper woodlands. Many of the lumberjacks who felled the forests of Ohio, Minnesota, and Michigan had their start in Maine.

In the 1850s a process for making paper out of wood pulp (as opposed to the traditional rags) was developed and a new market for softwood opened. By 1868 the first mill for manufacturing wood pulp in substantial quantities was built in Topsham, Maine. Over the next fifty years, pulp mills and their dams grew like mushrooms along every major river in the state, spewing tons of noxious wastes into once drinkable water. Meanwhile, other forms of forest exploitation were developing. One of the first mills in the country that mass-produced wood turnings using a new kind of mechanical lathe went into operation in Locke Mills in 1865. Within a few years, Maine led the nation in the production of broom handles, spindles, spools, and other turned-wood products. The push was on for wood—and more wood. "Cut the best and leave the rest!" was the logger's motto. By the late 1800s the "best" of what was left had been cut twice—even three times—in some places, leaving an unhealthy forest where logging had been heavy.

The uncut forest was resistant to insect and disease infestations because host trees of the right age for such blights never dominated any stand. It was resistant to fire because of its thick canopy and high moisture content, resistant to wind because it was bulwarked by massive old-growth trees, and the root system was stable and deep. With heavy cutting and uniform-age regrowth in depleted soil came the inevitable afflictions of a forest under stress: erosion, disease, insect infestation, wind damage, and fire. Maine's peak production for lumber was reached in 1909 at 1.1 billion board feet. A year later, a spruce budworm epidemic broke out that within a decade wiped out a large proportion of all spruce and fir in the state. During the same era, forest fires in the state claimed between one hundred fifty and two hundred fifty thousand acres each year.

The 1920s and 1930s saw a mild reprieve for the Maine Woods and other wildlands. Americans had become alarmed by the spiraling loss of wilderness across the nation, realizing nearly too late that the wilderness was not endless. The first substantial conservation movement blossomed. Huge tracts of wildlands were set aside as parks—including Baxter State Park, home of Mount Katahdin, which was donated to Maine by former Governor Percival Baxter—beginning in 1931. Some principles of forestry and game management became recognized and respected, and the problem of forest fires was finally seriously addressed. Maine, which built the first fire tower in the nation on Squaw Mountain in 1906, was a pioneer of forest-fire prevention. Although the forests had been severely overcut in many places, the cut-and-get-out philosophy of the nineteenth century was replaced, at least in theory, by a desire for sustainable timber. There simply was no more unexploited forest to move on to.

Into the 1940s, loggers in Maine still used horse teams and crosscut saws and bucksaws to cut wood, floating logs out of the forest over streams and rivers in spring.

Roads of any kind north of Moosehead Lake were all but nonexistent. Although lumbermen persisted in their genetically disastrous practice of taking the best, they observed a strict minimum girth guideline—usually sixteen inches—and generally did most of their logging in winter over snow and ice-shielded ground. From 1920 to 1950, nearly eighteen thousand farms in Maine were abandoned. Millions of acres were given a reprieve from the use of chemical fertilizer and pesticides and allowed to revert back to forest (much of this land still remains forest today). In the 1930s, times were tough for many, but a small logger with a sled and horse team could make a living for himself and his family. Life in the woods was still simple, isolated, and rugged.

Then came World War II and its technological boom. Into the woods came chain saws, skidders, and pulp trucks. At the same time, the nation's love affair with the automobile was consummated, giving birth to roads, roads, and more roads. The Maine Woods were no longer accessible to just loggers and adventurous sportsmen. From 1960 to the present, more change has come to the Maine Woods than in the entire three hundred fifty years following the founding of the ill-fated Popham Colony of 1608.

FROM KING'S MASTS TO BIOMASS

They have even descended to smaller game. They have, lately, as I hear, invented a machine for chopping up huckleberry bushes fine and so converting them into fuel!—bushes which, for fruit alone are worth all the pear trees in the country many times over.

Henry David Thoreau came to the Maine Woods just after the first roads had penetrated its virgin recesses. He found a forest already under siege. Trees were being stripped from the woods as fast as loggers could get to them. As wild and unbroken as most of Maine then was, Thoreau foresaw that it would not remain so under such exploitation. At this rate, he bitterly mused, "we shall be forced to gnaw the very crust of the earth for our nutriment."

When John Weymouth and his followers settled in Popham Beach in 1608, there were nearly twenty-one million acres of old-growth forest covering the state—virtually all but the tops of the tallest mountains, the marshes, and the sandy beaches in the south. Today, no virgin forest and less than seven thousand acres of

old-growth forest remain. More than half of this old-growth is still threatened by logging. The remaining forest, which even today covers eighty-five percent of the state, is third- and fourth-growth wood. The trees average a mere thirty-five years in age and eight inches in diameter, the smallest average diameter for forest trees of any state in the United States. The quality of these trees is considered by many professional foresters to be the poorest in the history of the Maine Woods. Forty-three percent of all hardwoods and thirty-seven percent of all softwoods are estimated to be diseased or otherwise unsound. The last spruce budworm epidemic wiped out as much as seventy-five percent of the mature fir in the northern half of the state, while in the past twenty years more than half of all red spruce above an elevation of twenty-five hundred feet have died because of the effects of acid rain or toxic wind. Nearly all mature beech in the Maine Woods is afflicted by an insect infestation that encrusts its smooth, silvery bark with ugly scabs, while the woolly aphid is a chronic threat to balsam fir and the white pine. The tent caterpillar has defoliated millions of maple and poplar over the past few decades. This forest is sick.

Yet the current cutting rate in Maine is roughly double the sustainable growth rate. While logging was once confined to the cold months, when roads were iced down for sledding logs out with horse teams and wood was "yarded" until the spring river drives, cutting now goes on almost year-round. In many places, cutting goes on around the clock. Younger and younger trees are being taken in the fever to meet the growing demand for wood, and the next "logical" step in this progression is now being taken: "whole-tree harvesting" or, more accurately, biomass chipping. Everything on a piece of land—entire trees, branches, and twigs, along with shrubs, saplings, and bushes—is shaved from the land and put through an on-site machine that reduces it all to wood chips. Trees do not have to be any particular size. Loggers can go back every ten to fifteen years and reharvest scrubby new growth. This form of harvesting threatens to become more common, because it is quicker and easier. Logs are no longer a prerequisite in the wood business.

Demand seems insatiable. While the United States is beginning to import more wood from Canada and the Brazilian rain forest where it is still plentiful and therefore cheap, it is at the same time tapping into the profits that can be made by exporting domestic wood to Europe, Japan, the Middle East, and other countries that have long since exhausted their own timber resources. Some nations are willing to pay two to three times more for wood than are Americans. Currently, orders for millions of board feet of wood are coming into Maine more quickly than trees can be felled, as the Maine forest is pressed to compensate for the lack of forest stewardship overseas. As scientists work to devise new products using wood fiber, including formerly petroleum-based synthetics, and as more energy-generating plants and factories that burn wood chips are built, cellulose—in just about any form—is the sole raw material that is required by the wood products industry.

However, under the nutrient-stripping conditions imposed by biomass chipping, no forest land can renew itself, and such land will eventually become barren or dangerously chemical-dependent. The forest soil, an almost nonrenewable resource, has already been severely depleted by erosion and compaction by logging machines that also remove renewing detritus (dead trees and slash). Pesticides have killed not only target insects but soil-renewing microbes and vital detritus-eaters such as beetles, worms, and ants.

Fertilizer used on lawns, farms, and tree plantations kills natural nitrogen-fixing microbes and changes the soil pH balance, drastically altering the soil habitat. Studies have shown that plants growing in depleted soil not only fail to thrive but do not reproduce as well as those in an unaltered habitat. In Maine, deer experts have discovered that the deer population in more heavily developed southern regions of the state, despite abundant food, are afflicted by a higher rate of disease than those in heavily forested regions to the north where the deer herd is virtually disease-free. It has also been found in a Washington state study that the browse that grows in clear-cuts is significantly reduced in nutritional content, which may have a negative impact on the health of the animals who rely on it. The soil condition in the northern forest lands seems dependent on the health of the forest to a great extent. The new forest of Maine, shallowly rooted in anemic, compacted soil, is vulnerable to a host of threats. At the Penobscot Experimental Forest in Bradley, the U.S. Forest Service found that the spruce-budworm infestation is far more severe in a single-age, single-species forest than it is in a natural, multi-age, multispecies woods. Yet the forest industry is encouraging the growth of more single-age, single-species forests than ever before by establishing "paper plantations" using clear-cutting. After clear-cutting, strong herbicides are sprayed on the land to kill hardwood "brush" such as raspberries, alders, and

other natural first colonists of deforested land—so only softwood can more rapidly emerge. Despite citizen opposition to the industry's growing dependence on herbicides, Maine uses six times more herbicide than any other logging region in the United States. In addition to the unknown long-term effects of such chemicals on flora and fauna, many professional foresters have noted that land on which herbicides have been used is far drier than land left to reforest itself naturally.

Mechanical harvesting causes soil compaction on more than ninety percent of the area being logged. Land damage increases proportionally with the size of the equipment being used and the amount of biomass removed. The soil nutrient depletion caused by clear-cutting and whole-tree harvesting is alarming. Studies have revealed that over a three-year period after it has been clear-cut, land loses as much as a quarter of a ton per acre of mineral nutrients (calcium, nitrate, magnesium, and potassium) to leaching and erosion. After whole-tree harvesting, this amount may run as high as three-quarters of a ton with increased acidity, erosion, and nutrient depletion found to persist even after eight years. Yet the industry continues to justify and promote increased use of whole-tree chipping and clear-cutting as "land management tools." The dramatic changes in the plant cover of the land are praised with seductive, but purely economic and finally specious, arguments. The open brushy areas and sapling woods caused by clear-cuts are touted by industry spokespersons and state wildlife officials as "good habitats" only because the species that tend to thrive there have some economic value to human beings: ruffed grouse, deer, and other birds and mammals that are commonly hunted and trapped.

A 1990 study revealed that paper companies are responsible for dumping more tons of pollutants into the air, water, and soil of New England than any other industrial source. By far, the bulk of this pollution could be traced to Maine mills. Although stricter regulations now prevent the dumping of dioxin-contaminated sludge directly into rivers, paper companies have recently adopted a more insidious and potentially far more lethal approach to the disposal of this sludge. It is now being trucked—by the *billions* of pounds—to remote forest land around Moosehead Lake, to be spread as "fertilizer" on clear-cuts. The affected region lies around the headwaters of several of Maine's major rivers. It is conceivable that in the future, entire rivers—only recently considered in their northernmost stretches to be among the purest in the nation—will become contaminated by dioxin, instead of only the sections below mills. Yet the state continues to look the other way.

Despite the growing number of state regulations on specific aspects of logging, arising from public clamor, the government refuses to regulate comprehensively the use of private forest land and has even refused to regulate most aspects of cutting in national forests. Even among the most farsighted state governments, only the most feeble, poorly enforced standards exist. Maine is no exception. Companies can, in other words, clear-cut as frequently as they wish as long as they build adequate skidder roads and leave a strip of trees bordering streams, lakes, and ponds. However, in the industrial forest, there is an average of only one professional forester hired to oversee the management of every one hundred seventy thousand acres of land. Management practices too are based on economic rather than environmental priorities or esthetic values. According to the *Forestry for Maine's Future* report (1988)—which echoes industry philosophy—red maple, the classic fiery tree of autumn, which has limited industrial use, is judged "not particularly valuable." Gray birch and alder, which compete with softwood growth after a clear-cut, are condemned as "junk species"; and old-growth trees, to promote their speedy harvest, are labeled "over-mature." The industrial staples, spruce and fir, are lauded as almost the only "appropriate species." The forest industry continually packages its more exploitive practices in glossy, misleading euphemisms. Killing hardwood growth with herbicides is called "releasing suppressed species" or "precommercial thinning." Clear-cutting and wood-chipping the forest is called "intensive management."

However, present forest practices are coming under increasing fire from the public, who, because of the new road system, are coming more often into the Maine Woods. The industry's response to the public outcry against the ugly scars of clear-cutting: Don't let loggers clear-cut within sight of roads. Yet the altering of silvicultural practices as a result of public outcry is unlikely to occur soon in Maine. *Maine at the Millennium: The Commission on Maine's Future*, a report released in the fall of 1989, observed that the state and federal governments exercise more control, with less citizen input, than ever before in the state's history, and that "our system of government has evolved into one based on top-down decision making at all levels of government, encouraging influence from special interests rather than diverse and active public participation." Nowhere does this hold more true than in issues involving the Maine Woods. With a population of only thirteen thousand in the state's "unorganized territories," a high percentage of whom fall well below the federal poverty line, and with well over half of the land in the region owned by a handful of paper companies, there is no question who carries the big stick in state politics.

The paper industry is showered with every tax break, grant, and subsidy that can be loosed from state coffers. Half of the members of the 1988 state "Citizens Forestry Advisory Council" were past and present industry employees or executives. In 1990 the governor's brother was a paper company lobbyist in Washington. The forest industry maintains, and has for decades, a stranglehold upon Maine's government.

THE LOGGER'S LIFE

Is it the lumberman, then, who is the friend and lover of the pine, stands nearest to it, and understands its nature best?

The life of a logger has never been easy. In the mid-1800s, lumberjacks lived half the year in all but inaccessible wilderness cabins with no amenities—not even beds, in many cases—and felled trees four or five feet in diameter with axes alone, sometimes at temperatures of thirty below. In spring they drove millions of logs down ice-water river rapids armed only with iron-tipped sticks, and they drowned with regularity. The logger's life was by rights the stuff of tall tales.

A century later, in the post–World War II era, woods work had become less spartan but, thanks to chain saws, still dangerous. Piece-work pay was instituted by the forest industry as a blanket "take it or leave it" proposition during the Depression and was not discontinued even in the more prosperous decades that followed. The early chain saws, which began to replace crosscut saws and bucksaws in

the 1950s, were huge, awkward devices weighing up to one hundred pounds each and requiring two men to operate. The first lighter-weight saws, on the other hand, were prone to fly apart while cutting. The new saws and piece-work pay proved a deadly combination as exhausted men pushed themselves to fell enough trees to make a paycheck. The accident rate was high: Throughout the 1970s, one out of every eight Maine Woods workers suffered disabling injuries each year, and twenty were killed in that decade.

Although most forest-product companies own much large machinery and maintain a corps of loggers on their payroll, the highest percentage of wood is cut by independent contractors. In the past thirty years, the trend has been for mills to buy wood in larger volume per purchase. In this system most small loggers can no longer sell their wood directly to the mills;

they must sell it first to a "wood buyer," who then sells it as part of a larger lot to the mills. These middlemen are also logging contractors who own their own large equipment and, using piece labor, cut constantly in order to supply part of their regular orders from the mills. Therefore, when wood demand is low at the mill, the small logger is squeezed out of the picture altogether. The wood buyers have become a powerful and prosperous force in the forest economy. However, it is the paper companies that ultimately control that economy. They set the stumpage rate contractors pay and the mill price they receive once the wood is cut. In the 1970s, paper companies, while claiming they could not afford to hire more loggers at an hourly rate or offer better prices at the mill, paid out millions of dollars in fines for price-fixing. In 1974, independent loggers organized a strike, refusing to deliver logs to the mills, but the state government intervened on behalf of paper companies and the strike was crushed.

By the late 1970s, when skidders had replaced most chain-saw teams, woods work became somewhat safer. Each skidder could do the work of half a dozen men. Over the past twenty years, although the annual volume of wood cut has doubled, the number of jobs in the woods has shrunk by nearly one-half. Despite the marginal increase in safety brought about by mechanical harvesting, loggers now face the more subtle risks of joblessness and poverty. The high rate of substance abuse, domestic violence, teen pregnancy, and other products of despair and poverty prevalent among families dependent on the forest economy has been poignantly outlined in government reports and news media features in Maine. The archaic piece-work system is still in place. One-quarter of all full-time loggers in Maine fall below the national poverty line. They are still subject to an accident rate three times as high as that for all other manufacturing jobs. The loggers who are managing to hang on must struggle beneath unbelievable overhead just to be able to compete. Skidders cost fifty thousand dollars and up; feller-bunchers (also called harvesters), which do the work of ten men, start at around two hundred thousand dollars; a whole-tree chipper runs half a million or more. The independent contractor must also pay his own ever-increasing insurance and workers' compensation bills as well as the inevitable repair bills.

Under such conditions, it is not surprising that many logging contractors believe they have neither the time nor money to spend meeting the poorly enforced state forestry regulations. A 1988 state conservation department report on forestry practices found that most violations of regulations were perpetrated by the smaller independent contractors. The worst scenarios involve clear-cutting, the quickest and most cost-effective way to turn trees into cash. "Shoddy clear-cutting and associated roadbuilding are all too common in Maine," the report lamented. "It is not forestry and it is certainly not land stewardship."

Although the forest industry invests huge sums annually on massive public-image campaigns, the paper companies still assert they cannot afford to assume the responsibility of hourly wages for loggers or to raise rates to reasonable levels. The average domestic price paid at a Maine mill for spruce or fir pulpwood in 1990 was only sixty dollars a cord. At that rate, a logger must cut perhaps twenty-five cords of wood just to make one skidder payment.

ROADS AND PEOPLE

But Maine, perhaps, will soon be where Massachusetts is. A good part of her territory is already as bare and commonplace as much of our neighborhood and her villages generally not so well shaded as ours.

The year Henry David Thoreau graduated from college, 1837, the first summer visitor was boarded in Old Orchard Beach, Maine, and the state's tourist industry was born. Enterprising Mainers early on realized the economic potential of the state's scenic beauty and abundant natural waterways, fish, and game, and encouraged visitors. Somewhat ironically, Thoreau's *Maine Woods*, along with other chronicles of travel through the northern forest (essays by Thoreau's "nemesis," James Russell Lowell, among them), helped give birth to the era of the Maine Woods sporting camp and inland tourism.

By 1884 the phrase "Maine, the Nation's Playground" had been coined by a Maine Central Railroad manager. The following year, the railroad issued the first guidebook for tourists. By then, nearly fifty thousand tourists were flocking to Maine each year. Although most were drawn to the coast, hundreds of hunters and fishermen went to the forest to stay in remote, but pampering, sporting camps. With logging camps relying on local game to supplement their larders and almost no serious regulations pertaining to game yet in existence (out-of-state hunters were not even required to purchase a license), the toll on the state's wildlife populations was severe. By 1873 the state had imposed the first bag limit on deer, two per hunter, to protect the rapidly dwindling herd. It was too late for the caribou. By 1900 the state's last "reindeer" had been shot. By then, moose were also threatened and were saved only by the more stringently enforced game laws of the twentieth century.

Although the Maine Woods were dubbed a "sportsman's paradise," the number of inland tourists was limited for a time by necessity. Railroads and stage roads only went so far. Travel further north was done almost entirely by canoes and bateaux over rivers and lakes. This was the stuff of romance, and the northern wilderness highly intrigued residents of New England and the urban East Coast, many of whom had already seen the last wildlands in their states fall under the logger's axe or the builder's pick and shovel. "Maine Woods" became synonymous with "wilderness."

Thanks to the automobile and its accompanying road system, the number of tourists coming to Maine annually rose from fifty thousand in the gay nineties to over six million in 1989. Although most tourism remains concentrated along the seacoast, more tourists are going inland than ever before. After the last log was driven down the state's rivers in 1974, the push was on to build good roads into the forests so skidders and pulp trucks could get in and out of timberland. In the last twenty-five years alone, over twenty thousand miles of road have been bulldozed through the forest, more than a third of all the road mileage in the state in a region that is home to only a hundredth of its population. These "logging roads" are not the narrow, rugged tracks of yore; they are wide, well-maintained forest "highways" along which any vehicle can freely travel year round. Tourists can now drive not just to Greenville, but to the Allagash and the most remote stretch of the St. John River. Thanks to this road system, the north

woods, once accessible only to the most dedicated sportsmen, is now just a leisurely day's drive away for sixty-five million people.

Although roads may be a blessing for the tourist industry, they are anathema to wildlands. Roads devour collectively large amounts of land—from about four acres per mile for a rural road to as much as two hundred acres per mile for a major highway. Logging roads in the Maine Woods cause erosion and dust pollution in dry weather. They lead to the sedimentation and frequent demise of nearby streams and ponds. In summer, the borders of these roads are sprayed routinely with herbicides, while in winter they are dosed with road salt. They are, in all seasons, receptacles for cumulatively significant amounts of diesel fuel, gasoline, motor oil, brake fluid, and trash (including lit cigarettes) from passing vehicles. They pose a major disruption for wildlife habitats as well as a lethal physical hazard to animals. Between thirty thousand and seventy-five thousand birds, reptiles, and mammals (including three thousand white-tailed deer) are killed on Maine roads each year.

Most important of all, these logging roads create access to the wildlands for larger numbers of people. The recreational use of the Maine Woods has been increasing at a rate of five percent annually and, with it, the frequency of vandalism, forest fires, and littering. The latter is one of the most ubiquitous—and damaging—forms of wildland pollution. The degree of the problem is invariably underestimated—or overlooked altogether. Over forty pounds of trash per mile was recovered in a 1987 study along the relatively "unspoiled" shores of Maine's Lake Cobbossecontee. Half of the total weight consisted of plastics: Styrofoam cups, plastic bags, lids, diapers, beer and soda can rings, fishing line, and fishing "bobbers." This casually discarded trash becomes an ecological minefield for wildlife. Shorebirds frequently become tangled in fishing line and are crippled or drowned in their struggles to escape—or they eventually starve. Untold numbers of fish slowly die after ingesting small bits of floating plastic, while small mammals and birds are regularly strangled by plastic beer and soda rings. As most of this garbage is nonbiodegradable, the level of hazard grows annually. Even the so-called biodegradable plastics remain viable—and dangerous to wildlife—for several months.

This overuse and disruptive use of the wildlands resources is fast changing the character of the north woods. Streams that were once fished by only a handful of local residents are now lined by sportsmen from Memorial Day through Labor Day, and the average size of the catch is declining yearly. Small ponds once accented only by the cry of a loon now resound with the roar of high-speed motorboats, jet skis, and boom boxes. Narrow trails once used just by hikers and moose are now deeply eroded thoroughfares for all-terrain vehicles and dirt bikes.

As real estate on the seacoast becomes inaccessible to all but the wealthiest, another pressure on the Maine Woods is being felt: development. As many north woods natives struggle to hold on to their homes, more affluent southern Mainers and people from other states are buying up prime forest land—much of it on lakes and ponds—and building second homes. In 1988, out of the eleven thousand houses standing in the state's unorganized townships, only three thousand were year-round dwellings. The rest were vacation homes used only a few weeks each year. Unlike with logging, the environmental changes and loss of wildlife habitat imposed by development may be completely irreversible. With development comes roads, power and phone lines, septic systems, buried oil and gas tanks, landfills, stores, and water lines. Subtler effects are also felt, such as light, noise and heat pollution, and domestic pets. In many regions more deer kills can be traced to domestic dogs than to coyotes and bobcats combined, while cats can have a significant impact on local populations of squirrel, bird, and chipmunk. Developed land is also toxic land: More chemical pesticide and fertilizer is used on each acre of American lawn and garden than on any other type of land, including farmland and industrial forests. Despite tighter state regulations of septic systems, hundreds of Maine Woods homes, especially seasonal camps, still spew sewage directly into the nearest water body. Because most forest animals spend their entire lives within a territory of twenty acres or more, upon which they must depend for food and water and across which they must regularly travel, multiple small pieces of privately owned land that has been developed cut more sharply into wildlife habitats and ranges than do the larger tracts owned by the state and by paper companies.

CONSUMING THE WILDERNESS

And what are we coming to? . . .The very willow rows lopped every three years for fuel or powder, and every sizeable pine and oak or other forest tree cut down within the memory of man! As if individual speculators were to be allowed to export the clouds out of the sky or the stars out of the firmament. . . .

Although the modern forest industry now uses as much of each tree cut as possible, the waste of timber resources is just as rampant as ever. In the past, waste took the form of discarded hemlock or pine trees left lying in the forest. Today it takes the form of finished products lying on a trash heap. In 1988 Americans discarded sixty-six million tons of paper and cardboard. Wastepaper and cardboard make up over forty percent of the solid waste generated in this country annually. Three-quarters of this mountain of discarded paper and cardboard is packaging, twenty-five million tons of which is purely cosmetic and nonessential. Each year every man, woman, and child in America purchases and discards an average of six hundred fifty pounds of packaging.

The toll that our highly consumptive lifestyle takes upon the nation's forests is staggering. Each year, enough trees to re-forest a land area nearly the size of Connecticut wind up in municipal landfills and incinerators in the form of wastepaper, cardboard, and wood. The trees felled solely to produce packaging material every year would reforest an area the size of Delaware. Sustaining such a rate of consumption seems impossible, yet demand for paper products—especially packaging—continues to grow. In spite of the growth of electronic data processing, humans have a ravenous appetite for paper. "Paperwork" of all varieties permeates modern life. The amount of paper added each year to the file cabinets of government offices, insurance companies, banks, schools, medical care providers, and other organizations rivals the amount discarded by these institutions each year. Some daily newspapers, colossal consumers of paper, are shifting to "virgin" pulp, rather than using recycled newsprint, because of new color reproduction processes. This shift alone is a heavy blow to the forest: Each week over half a million trees fall just to provide Americans with their Sunday newspapers. Today, only about twelve percent of all those papers are recycled. Other growing sources of nonrecyclable paper wastes are coupons; fliers; "glossy" magazines; and most bleached, wax-coated, or corrugated paper and cardboard cartons. Ironically, the volume of paper being recycled, according to the American Paper Institute, is actually growing steadily. But the volume of paper products being consumed is growing more rapidly, canceling out any net gain to the forest.

The American demand for paper is so great that our logging industry cannot cut fast enough to keep up with it. Millions of cords of wood must be imported from Canada and other forested countries. Americans are unlikely to change their pattern of consumption as long as paper is held so cheap. And as long as paper is cheap, the nation's forests—and the Maine Woods—will be held cheap as well. Today a ream of typing paper can be purchased for as little as two dollars (wholesale), and each year billions of paper towels, plates, cups, and napkins, all produced to be discarded, are sold for mere pennies apiece. Packaging is rarely even considered part of a consumer purchase. Our wood-pulp-based luxuries have become necessities— worse yet, routine—and for too many Americans, the forest is a remote entity, the wilderness a myth. It is little wonder that the connection between material goods and the natural resources that are used to produce them is being lost—and with it, our last wildlands.

PART FOUR

CONTACT!
A Photographic Odyssey
through
the Maine Woods

With excerpts from the journals of
HENRY DAVID THOREAU

Now we behold those features which the discoverers saw, apparently unchanged.

Moosehead Lake

Nature here was something savage and awful, though beautiful. This was that Earth of which we have heard, made out of Chaos and Old Night. Here was no man's garden, but the unhandselled globe. It was not lawn, nor pasture, nor mead, nor wood-land, nor lea, nor arable, nor wasteland. It was the fresh and natural surface of the planet Earth.

Clouds surround Mount Katahdin

There was here felt the presence of a force not bound to be kind to man.

Fisher tracks—Spectacle Pond near Monson

Only solemn, bear-haunted mountains, with their great wooded slopes were visible, where, as man is not, we suppose some other power to be . . . and yet I was tempted to walk there.

Sunrise over Moosehead Lake

Talk of mysteries! Think of our life in nature, daily to be shown matter, to come in contact with it—rocks, trees, wind on our cheeks! The solid *earth! The* actual *world!* Contact! Contact! Who *are we?* Where *are we?*

Mountain stream, Penobscot County

The moose will perhaps one day become extinct, but how naturally then, when it exists only as a fossil relic, and unseen at that, may the poet or sculptor invent a fabulous animal with similar branching and leafy horns—a sort of fucus or lichen in bone—to be the inhabitant of such a forest as this!

Bull moose, Baxter State Park

*There are not only stately
pines, but fragile flowers . . .
which derive their nutriment
from the crudest mass of peat.
These remind us that not only
for strength, but for beauty,
the poet must, from time to
time, travel the logger's path
and the Indian's trail, to drink
at some new and more brac-
ing fountain of the Muses, far
in the recesses of the wilderness.*

Fringed polygola (milkwort family)

And in that fresh, cool atmosphere, the hylodes were peeping and the toads ringing about the lake universally as in the spring. It was as if the season had revolved backward two or three months, or I had arrived at the abode of perpetual spring.

Pickerel weed

There is something singularly grand and impressive in the sound of a tree falling in a perfectly calm night like this, as if the agencies which overthrow it did not need to be excited but worked with a subtle, deliberate and conscious force . . .

West branch, Penobscot River

It is difficult to conceive of a region uninhabited by man. We habitually presume his presence and influence everywhere. And yet we have not seen pure nature unless we have seen her thus, vast and drear and inhuman . . . though in the midst of cities.

Dawn, Mount Katahdin

The mountain seemed a vast aggregation of loose rocks, as if sometime it had rained rocks and they lay as they fell on the mountainsides. They were the raw materials of a planet dropped from an unseen quarry, which the vast chemistry of nature would anon work up or work down into the smiling and verdant plains and valleys of earth.

Baxter State Park viewed from Mount Katahdin's Hunt Trail

It was vast, Titanic, and such as man never inhabits. Some part of the beholder, even some vital part, seems to escape through the loose grating of his ribs as he ascends. He is more lone than you can imagine. His reason is dispersed and shadowy, more thin and subtle, like the air. Vast, Titanic, inhuman Nature has got him at a disadvantage, caught him alone, and pilfers him of some of his divine faculty.

Moosehead Lake, from Mount Kineo

It was the most wild and desolate region we had camped in, where, if anywhere, one might expect to meet with befitting inhabitants, but I heard only the squeak of a nighthawk flitting over.

Telos Lake

Only some utterly uncivilized, big-throated owl hooted loud and dismally in the drear and boughy wilderness, plainly not afraid to hear the echoes of his voice.

Cow moose, Pleasant River

It was ready to echo the growl of a bear, the howl of a wolf, or the scream of a panther. But when you get fairly into the middle of one of these grim forests, you are surprised to find that the larger inhabitants are not at home commonly, but have left only a puny red squirrel to bark at you. Generally speaking, a howling wilderness does not howl: it is the imagination of the traveler that does the howling.

Chipmunk

The tops of the mountains are among the unfinished parts of the globe, wither it is a slight insult to the gods to climb and pry into their secrets and try their effect on our humanity.

Logging truck on the "Golden Road"

If I wished to see a mountain or other scenery under the most favorable auspices, I would go to it in foul weather, so as to be there when it cleared up; we are then in the most suitable mood and nature is most fresh and inspiring. There is no serenity so fair as that which is just established in a tearful eye.

Thoreau's Island—upper west branch, Penobscot River

They are sometimes used for ornamental hat trees, together with deer's horns, in front entries . . . I trust that I shall have a better excuse for killing a moose than that I may hang my hat on his horns.

Moose horns on a lamppost—crossroads
between Abbot and Monson

I let science slide and rejoiced. . . . I believed that the woods were not tenantless, but choked full of honest spirits as good as myself any day, not an empty chamber in which chemistry was left to work alone, but an inhabited house . . . and for a few moments I enjoyed fellowship with them.

Lobster Lake

I little thought there was such a light shining in the darkness of the wilderness for me.

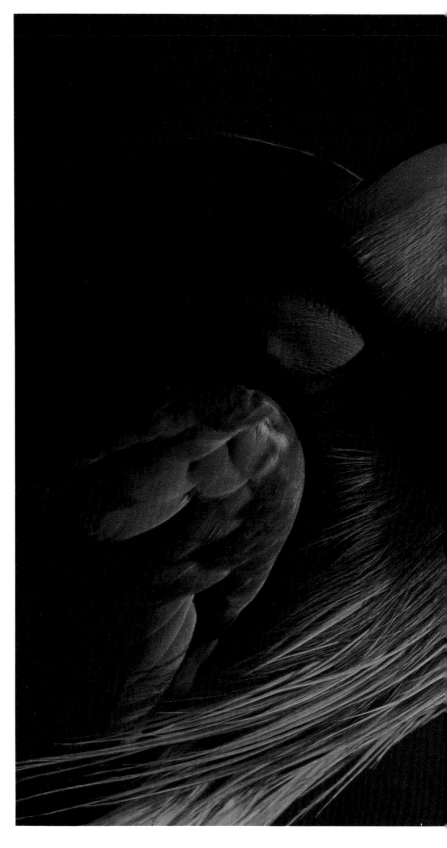

Great blue heron

What a wilderness walk for a man to take alone! None of your half-mile swamps; none of your milewide woods merely, as on the skirts of our towns; without hotels; only a dark mountain or a lake for guideboard and station.

The Maine Woods from Mount Katahdin

Strange that so few ever come to the woods to see how the pine lives and grows and spires, lifting its evergreen arms to the light, to see its perfect success, but most are content to behold it in the shape of many broad boards brought to market and deem that its true success!

White pine stump

For one that comes with a pencil to sketch, or to sing, a thousand come with an axe or rifle.

Discarded limbs and trunks

The woods were as fresh and full of vegetable life as a lichen in wet weather and contained many interesting plants, but unless they are of white pine, they are treated with as little respect here as a mildew, and in the other case, they are only the more quickly cut down.

Waterfall near Rangeley

Our life should be lived as tenderly and daintily as one would pluck a flower.

White pine sprig

A belt of dead trees stood all around the lake, and they made the shore, for the most part, inaccessible. Thus they had dammed all the larger lakes, raising their broad surfaces many feet, thus turning the forces of Nature against herself that they might float their spoils out of the country. Think how much land they have flowed without asking Nature's leave!

Driftwood—northern shore,
Chamberlain Lake

This hunting of the moose merely for the satisfaction of killing him—not even for the sake of his hide—without making any extraordinary exertion or running any risk yourself, is too much like going out by night to some woodside pasture and shooting your neighbor's horses. They are God's own horses, poor timid creatures, that will run fast enough as soon as they smell you, though they are nine feet high.

Yearling moose

Standing on a mountain in the midst of a lake, where would you look for the first sign of approaching fair weather? Not into the heavens, it seems, but into the lake.

Forest pond, Piscataquis County

Blissful, innocent Nature, like a serene infant, is too happy to make a noise, except by a few tinkling, lisping birds and trickling rills.

Katahdin Stream Falls, Baxter State Park

They bore a certain propor-
tion to the great Moosehead
Lake on whose bosom they
floated and I felt as if they
were under its protection.

Loon on Little Lyford Pond,
Piscataquis County

129

It was always startling to discover so plain a trail of civilized man there.

Slate pit in Monson—now used as a dump

Wild as it was, it was hard for me to get rid of the associations of human industry. The waterfalls which I heard were not without their dams and mills to my imagination, and several times I found I had been regarding the steady rushing of the wind from over the woods beyond the rivers as that of a train of cars.

Waterfall

He who rides and keeps the beaten track studies the fences chiefly.

Recreational vehicles, Allagash
Wilderness Waterway

I even thought that a row of wigwams with a dance of powwows and a prisoner tortured at the stake would be more respectable than this.

Rafters on the west branch of the Penobscot River

The Indian said that the caribou was a "very great runner," that there were none about this lake now, though there used to be many, and pointing to the belt of dead trees caused by the dams, he added, "He no likum stump— when he see that, he scared."

Driftwood tree, Telos Lake

How far men go for the materials of their houses! The inhabitants of the most civilized cities in all ages send into far, primitive forests, beyond the bounds of their civilization, where the moose and bear and savage dwell, for their pine boards for ordinary use. On the other hand, the savage soon receives from cities, iron arrow points, hatchets and guns to point his savageness with.

Paper mill on the Androscoggin River

We do not suspect how much our chimneys have concealed.

Campfire

When the chopper would praise a pine, he would commonly tell you that the one he cut was so big that a yoke of oxen stood on its stump. Why, my dear sir, the tree might have stood on its own stump, and a deal more comfortably and firmly than a yoke of oxen can, if you had not cut it down. What right have you to celebrate the virtues of the man you have murdered?

Pulp truck

*But the pine is no more
lumber than man is, and to be
made into boards and houses
is no more its true and highest
use than the truest use of man
is to be cut down and made
into manure.*

Feller-buncher ("harvester") near the
Allagash Wilderness Waterway

146

Here were thousands of cords, enough to keep the poor of Boston or New York amply warm for a winter, which only cumbered the ground. . . . And the whole of that solid and interminable forest is doomed to be gradually devoured thus by fire, like shavings, and no man be warmed by it.

Pulp logs outside a paper mill

Through this steel riddle, more or less coarse, is the arrowy Maine forest, from Katahdin and Chesuncook and the headwaters of the St. John relentlessly sifted, till it comes out boards, clapboards, laths and shingles such as the wind can take, still, perchance, to be slit and slit again till men get a size that will suit.

Paper mill in western Maine

Think how stood the white pine tree . . . its branches sough-ing with the four winds and every individual needle trem-bling in the sunlight. Think how it stands with it now—sold, perchance, to the New England Friction Match Company!

Pulp truck near Millinocket

The very willow-rows lopped every three years for fuel or powder, and every sizeable pine and oak or other forest tree cut down within the memory of man! As if individual speculators were to be allowed to export the clouds out of the sky or the stars out of the firmament, one by one. We shall be reduced to gnaw the crust of the earth for nutriment.

Logging operation near Moosehead Lake

We shall be obliged to import the timber for our liberty pole—as leafless as it is fruit-less—or hereafter splice together such sticks as we have, and our ideas of liberty are equally mean with these.

Logs line the "Golden Road," south of Baxter State Park

It is war against the pines, the only real Aroostook or Penobscot war.

Logging operation near Moosehead Lake

The mission of men there seems to be, like so many busy demons, to drive the forest out of all the country, from every solitary beaver swamp and mountainside, as soon as possible.

Clear-cuts along the "Golden Road"

The wilderness experiences a sudden rise of all her streams and lakes, she feels ten thousand vermin gnawing at the base of her noblest trees, many combining, drag them off, jarring over the roots of the survivors, and tumble them into the nearest stream, till the fairest having fallen, they scamper off to ransack some new wilderness, and all is still again.

Paper mill near Rumford

163

CONTACT! A PHOTOGRAPHIC ODYSSEY

The moon in her first quarter, in the fore part of the night, setting over the bare rocky hills garnished with tall charred and hollow stumps or shells of trees, served to reveal the desolation.

Trees flooded by damming near Gulf Hagas

Here, then, one could no longer accuse institutions and society, but must front the true source of evil.

Clear-cut, north of Moosehead Lake

I have been into the lumberyard and the carpenter's shop and the tannery and the lampblack factory and the turpentine clearing. But when at length I saw the tops of the pines waving and reflecting the light at a distance high over all the rest of the forest, I realized that the former were not the highest uses of the pine. It is not their bones or hide or tallow that I love most; it is the living spirit of the tree, not its spirit of turpentine, with which I sympathize.

It is as immortal as I am and perchance will go to as high a heaven, there to tower above me still.

White pines at sunset

A pine cut down, a dead pine, is no more a pine than a dead human carcass is a man.

"Skidder" in a clear-cut

Every creature is better alive than dead, men and moose and pine trees, and he who understands it aright will rather preserve its life than destroy it.

White-tailed doe near Borestone
Mountain near Monson

173

The kings of England formerly had their forests "to hold the king's game," for sport or food, sometimes destroying villages to create or extend them. . . . Why should not we, who have renounced the king's authority, have our national preserves, where no villages need be destroyed, in which the bear and panther and even some of the hunter race may still exist and not be "civilized off the face of the earth . . .?"

Logging road, Piscataquis County

What a place to live, what a place to die and be buried in!

Traditional Abenaki Earth Day
ceremony on Cadillac Mountain

AFTERWORD

THE SOLUTION

*Every creature is better alive than dead, men and moose
and pine trees, and he who understands it aright will
rather preserve its life than destroy it.*

So what is the solution to the "problem of the wilderness"?

Before a solution can be found, the underlying problem must be identified. Pollution, alteration and destruction of habitat, and overuse by people threaten the wilderness, yet are merely symptoms of a deeper illness, an illness caused by deeply ingrained human attitudes. Beneath our everyday practices, especially in our patterns of consumption, there still runs a murky current of belief that people have dominance over the earth and that its resources are without limit.

Strengthening this belief, modern technology has placed an ever-thickening wall between humans and the source of all raw resources, nature. We take for granted the billions of tons of typing paper, two-by-fours, plywood, and newspapers that are part of daily life, yet rarely associate these products with the forests from which

they come. We see the water that springs from our taps or flushes away in our toilets, but rarely consider the lakes, springs, and rivers from which the water comes and to which it returns, all too often tainted. Thanks to science we now have the ability to free ourselves from the effects of the elements. We need not be wet or cold, hungry or in pain, or engulfed by darkness. And yet, like Thoreau, we sense that something is lacking—some unknown force we do not understand and therefore have been unable to harness. For Thoreau, it was not until his brother's death and the ensuing feelings of ultimate loss touched his life that he found at last what was missing from his life: wilderness, the untamed force of nature, unbound by man.

To bridge this growing gap between humans and the natural world and fill the deepening void in our modern lives, it is imperative that all people have responsi-

181

bly controlled, nonexploitive access to wildlands and accurate, enlightening information concerning them. Today's national forests, state parks, sanctuaries, and other wildlands, and the work of environmental writers, researchers, film-makers, and others are vital not just to the survival of the physical earth, but to the survival of man's spirit. Yet, at present, only two percent of the federal budget is allotted to wildlands acquisition and natural resources, while the media is largely given to consumption, not conservation.

The environment, especially in times of economic stress, is considered a low priority on a list of disordered priorities. The economy has long dictated our state and national environmental policies as well as our personal attitudes. Yet any fixes we apply to our economic problems are temporary, partial at best, and of value to but a few. There will always be new economic problems, but the wildlands that are set aside now and preserved are of value to everyone forever.

Upon the survival of the Maine Woods rest, indirectly, the survival of wildlands all over the globe. If Thoreau's forest falls, the wood products companies will simply move on to the next unexploited forest: to Canada, South America, Africa. If the cycle of destruction can be broken in Maine, the oldest "working forest" in the United States, there is hope it can be broken anywhere. The fate of the Maine Woods will likely become a precedent for all regions across the nation where forestland is threatened.

By far the most secure means to preserve wildlands is to permanently remove them from the economic market. But the public's acquiring land and creating national and state parks, forests, and sanctuaries alone is not safeguard enough. Because of the tremendous lobbying power of the forest industry, even public land is not safe from the logger's axe. Big business is actually aided and abetted in this exploitation by the very agency designed to protect wildlands: the national Forest Service. In the Ralph Nader study group report on national forests, *The Last Stand*, author Daniel Barney concluded that "pressured by the timber industry, the national Forest Service has been substituting a new respect for the timber dollar for its old respect for the land." The report was published in 1974. Since then, clear-cutting on federal land has been increasing annually. In Maine, three hundred thousand of the four hundred fifty thousand acres of the state's so-called public lands are being turned over to logging interests. Through the manipulation of the state's muddy directive to manage these lands for "multiple use," timber cutting has been designated the dominant use of these lands. Wildlife habitat and public enjoyment are considered secondary uses at best.

The current proposal by the Wilderness Society to set 2.7 million acres of Maine wildlands aside as a public reserve also espouses the concept of multiple use, yet designates wildlife habitat—the natural use—as dominant, followed by public recreation. Closely monitored selective timber cutting would constitute but a peripheral use. Since its founding in 1935 by former foresters Aldo Leopold and Bob Marshall, the Wilderness Society has been responsible for identifying and overseeing the acquisition of more wildlands than any other private nonprofit organization in the world. It has now turned its attention—not too late, it is hoped—to the plight of the Maine Woods. Its proposed Maine Woods Reserve would safeguard not only the future of Thoreau's beloved forest but undoubtedly the economic future of Maine Woods residents as well. The reserve would shift the region from a logging economy to a recreation and conservation economy. Timber cutting would continue, but on a strictly limited basis, while new jobs such as foresters, park rangers, public relations personnel, wildlife biologists, trail crews, and a host of others would be created. For many Mainers, the concept of setting aside 2.7 million acres seems exorbitant. Yet that represents less than one-tenth of all the wildlands that were in Maine—and undisturbed—before the coming of the white man. This is a small gesture of return in light of what has been taken from the forest since 1608.

The Maine Woods have always been a symbol of wildlands for urban easterners. Thoreau's essays have been read perhaps most eagerly by those Americans who have never seen, and may never see, the northern forest. Today, for people who live in the suburbs and cities of the eastern megalopolis, just the knowledge that a wilderness still exists within reach provides an emotional oasis of hope and reassurance in the midst of their high-pressure, technology-bound lives.

Like the rest of us, Thoreau was far from perfect. He was self-absorbed, stubborn, inconsistent, and judgmental. But he was also sensitive, kindhearted, acutely perceptive, and fiercely independent of thought. He longed to break free from all convention and live the transcendental ideal of "unto thine own self be true," yet he could never bring himself to permanently abandon the comforts of his parents' "modern" home or to pursue any cause beyond the perimeters of safety. He was, in short, a contradiction and a paradox—just like the rest of us.

Thoreau's greatest success lies not in his discovery of nature, so beautifully chronicled in his journals and books, but in his endless quest of it. He never stopped searching for deeper reaches of truth within himself, in others, and in the world. His greatest revelation, the one he has since shared with the entire world in the pages of his books, is that the deepest truths can be found not in scientific and religious doctrine, but in nature, whose purest form is wilderness.

It was in Maine that Thoreau finally found wilderness, in Maine that he touched his deepest truths.